REGULATING THE REGULATORS

REGULATING THE REGULATORS

An Introduction to the
Legislative Oversight
of Administrative
Rulemaking

James R. Bowers

New York
Westport, Connecticut
London

Library of Congress Cataloging-in-Publication Data

Bowers, James R.
    Regulating the regulators : an introduction to the legislative
oversight of administrative rulemaking / James R. Bowers.
      p. cm.
    Includes bibliographical references.
    ISBN 0–275–93354–7 (alk. paper)
    1. Administrative procedure—United States. 2. Legislative
oversight—United States. 3. Administrative procedure—Illinois.
4. Legislative oversight—Illinois. I. Title.
KF5411.B69   1990
342.73'066—dc20
[347.30266]   89–36697

Library of Congress Catalog Card Number: 89–36697
ISBN: 0–275–93354–7

First published in 1990

Praeger Publishers, One Madison Avenue, New York, NY 10010
An imprint of Greenwood Publishing Group, Inc.

Printed in the United States of America

The paper used in this book complies with the Permanent
Paper Standard issued by the National Information Standards
Organization (Z39.48–1984).

10 9 8 7 6 5 4 3 2 1

To the memory of Molly Suzanne. Though you lived but a few brief minutes, you taught me much about myself.

Contents

Tables

Preface

Since at least the 1970s, state legislatures have been confronted with a steady growth in the level of administrative discretion exercised by their state bureaucracies. The rapid growth in the volume of state regulations is one aspect of administrative discretion with which state legislatures have been increasingly confronted. This increased rulemaking activity threatens to rival, or even replace, state legislatures as the principal source of new laws emanating from state government.

To combat this alarming development, state legislatures now routinely seek to regain their preeminence over lawmaking by influencing and overseeing agency implementation of administrative rulemaking authority. This oversight is frequently conducted through a process commonly known as "rules review." Rules review is a routinized and systematic form of legislative oversight that encourages the responsible exercise of rulemaking authority by requiring legislative scrutiny of proposed regulations prior to their final adoption and implementation by the issuing agencies. The main purpose of this book is to present an introduction to this increasingly important method of how state legislatures are likely to go about "regulating the regulators."

From the moment the idea for this book was conceived as a research project to its publication, nearly five years have elapsed.

During the course of these years, a large number of people have contributed to its development and completion. Among these persons who deserve public acknowledgment is Beth Phillips, a good friend and former employee of the Illinois General Assembly, Joint Committee on Administrative Rules. She sparked my initial interest and appreciation that this special form of legislative oversight warranted closer investigation.

Intellectually, I am indebted to Irene Rubin, Gary Glenn, and David Everson for their sustained support, enthusiasm, and scholarly direction. Throughout the years, they have shown me much about the "art" of political science.

My wife, Jan, also deserves a great deal of credit for the completion of this book. She read and patiently edited the manuscript several times. More importantly, with but few complaints, she tolerated my workaholic tendencies throughout both the research and writing of this book, and I thank her for this.

Many other people deserve acknowledgment. First, Morris Ogul and Frederick Kaiser have been very supportive and shown interest in my work on rules review. In addition, Virginia Shogren deserves thanks for her constant typing and retyping of the manuscript. Northern Illinois University Graduate School and St. John Fisher Summer Grants Committee deserve acknowledgment for providing financial support throughout various stages of the research and writing of this book. I would also like to acknowledge Mary Glenn, my editor at Praeger, who saw merit in my original proposal and manuscript, and who moved quickly to acquire it for publication. I am also deeply indebted to those persons who consented to be interviewed for this study. This book would not have been possible without their willingness to allow me to intrude into their world and place it under academic scrutiny.

REGULATING THE
REGULATORS

1

Introduction

Social, economic, and technological advances of the twentieth century place demands upon legislatures for lawmaking in a broad array of policy areas that they neither envisioned nor are necessarily competent to address (West 1985, 19). In response to these new demands, Congress and the state legislatures increasingly redelegate lawmaking power as rulemaking authority to administrative agencies for formulating, implementing, and executing public policy (Lyons and Thomas 1978, 1). Through this redelegation, administrative agencies become a principal, perhaps the primary, source of new laws at both the state and national levels of government. For example, one recent commentator observed that the number of federal regulations issued in recent years has been as high as 7,000 annually, whereas Congress on average only enacts 300 public laws per year (Bryner 1987, 10). State governments have also witnessed a skyrocketing rate in the number of regulations issued. For example, in 1986 Illinois state agencies promulgated 698 regulations. These rules represented a 48 percent increase in the number of regulations filed since 1978 (Joint Committee on Administrative Rules [JCAR], Illinois General Assembly 1987). California state agencies in the fiscal year 1978–79 issued nearly 1,200 regulations (Starr 1980). In Georgia between 1971 and 1975, state agencies adopted 4,447 new or amended rules while the state legislature passed only 2,000 bills and resolutions (Hamm and Robertson 1981).

The regulations adopted by administrative agencies enjoy a legal standing equivalent to those laws passed by legislatures but without their public scrutiny or accountability. Like statutes passed by the legislature, they influence individual, group, or institutional behavior; redefine private rights and obligations; and, if violated, result in government services or benefits being withheld (Lyons and Thomas 1978, 1). But unlike legislative lawmaking, administrative rulemaking potentially conflicts with two principles of constitutional government: (1) separation of powers; and (2) representative government. To insure that these constitutional principles are maintained, administrative agencies need to exercise their rulemaking authority responsibly. Without the responsible exercise of rulemaking authority, it is possible that constitutional government will be replaced by bureaucratic government, and its citizens transformed from *homo civicus* to captives, clients, and antagonists of the administrative state (Nachmias and Rosenbloom 1980; Rosenbloom 1983).

One way to promote administrative responsibility is to make agencies externally responsible, or accountable, to the constitutionally recognized branches of government for the regulations they promulgate. The legislative oversight of administrative rulemaking or rules review is an increasingly popular tool used by state legislatures to secure this responsibility. Rules review has no direct counterpart in Congress. It provides for the prior review, or in some instances the prior approval, of proposed regulations by a state legislature before the rules can be formally adopted by the issuing agency. Though by no means entirely politically neutral, advocates of rules review assert that it is chiefly a legalistic oversight process that can be used for determining whether proposed regulations exceed their statutory authority and accurately reflect legislative intent (Ethridge 1985, 28; National Conference of State Legislatures [NCSL] 1979, 7).

THREE BASIC QUESTIONS

Since the middle 1970s, state legislatures have increasingly relied upon rules review to make state agencies accountable for their rulemaking. This increased use of rules review has not been matched by an equivalent academic interest in it. Only recently has any real interest among academics begun to develop (Bowers 1988; Ethridge 1984a, 1984b, 1985; Hamm and Robertson 1981; Mahoney 1985; Miller 1987).

The broad purpose of this study is to expand the academic scrutiny that rules review is now beginning to receive. It asks and attempts to answer three basic questions about rules review. An important first question is: Why is a state legislature likely to adopt a rules review process? Second, what is the substance and the nature of the accountability a legislature is likely to seek from state agencies through rules reviews? This question is also concerned with important characteristics of the rules review process that seem to explain the accountability actually sought, and to whom state agencies are made accountable. Third, what factors are likely to explain agency responsiveness to rules review? In most state legislatures, the rules review committee's authority is usually advisory. Under this condition, the accountability that is actually achieved through rules review depends on the state agencies' voluntary compliance with the committee's review. Whether the agencies actually comply is likely to depend upon a number of factors such as the "cost" of compliance.

RESEARCH SETTING

To examine the three questions discussed above, a case study of the rules review process in the Illinois General Assembly is presented for the purpose of developing analytic generalizations applicable to future analysis. The data for this case study are a series of interviews with principal and continuing participants in the Illinois rules review process and content analysis of such relevant documents as legislative debates, transcripts of committee meetings, and agency rulemaking files. A detailed discussion of the methodology employed throughout this study is presented in the Appendix.

In Illinois, the Joint Committee on Administrative Rules (JCAR) is responsible for rules review. Technically JCAR is not a legislative committee but a legislative service agency. Its membership is bipartisan and consists of 12 legislators. The members of JCAR are chosen by the Speaker of the Illinois House of Representatives, the president of the Illinois Senate, and the minority leaders from each chamber of the General Assembly. Each legislative leader chooses three members of the committee. The legislators designated to sit on JCAR serve two-year terms that coincide with the legislative session. Appointment to the committee is in addition to the members' regular legislative committee assignments (Legislative Research Unit [LRU], Illinois General Assembly 1984, 63).

JCAR's authority, and the scope of its review, are derived from the Illinois Administrative Procedure Act (IAPA). JCAR is empowered to review all forms of rulemaking undertaken by the Illinois state agencies—general, emergency, and peremptory. The Committee's review of these rules ranges from scrutinizing their statutory authority to reducing the number and bulk of regulations. JCAR is also empowered to evaluate and report on all rules in terms of their public policy.

JCAR's authority is principally advisory. What accountability it actually obtains from the state agencies is the result of their voluntary compliance with its objections. The main recourse JCAR has to an agency's refusal to modify or withdraw a regulation is to introduce corrective legislation that addresses the reasons for JCAR's initial objection to the proposed rule. In extreme cases, JCAR may also initiate the first step in issuing a legislative veto of an objectionable rule. If agreed to by three-fifths of the committee members, JCAR can issue a Prohibition Against Filing to a proposed regulation. This notification suspends the regulation for 180 days. For the suspension to become permanent, a joint resolution must pass in both houses of the General Assembly.

To assist it in its task of reviewing agency regulations, JCAR has a full-time professional staff of 26 headed by an executive director and two deputy directors. There are two divisions—the rules review and compliance division and the policy, planning, and administrative division—each with its own manager who reports to one of the deputy directors. The rules review and compliance division is further divided by the type of administrative rules reviewed. Within these subject areas are assigned both staff attorneys and rules analysts (JCAR 1986, 6).

CHAPTER OUTLINE

The remaining chapters in this study are primarily shaped around the three questions previously discussed. Chapter 2 lays the foundation for the rest of the study by placing rules review into the theoretical perspective of constitutional government. The three questions are answered in Chapters 3 through 6. Chapter 3 examines why a state legislature is likely to establish a rules review process by detailing the development of rules review in the Illinois General Assembly. Chapter 4 looks at the nature of rules review and the accountability actually sought through it. Chapter 5 examines the bureaucratic responsiveness to rules review and the accountability actually achieved through this responsiveness.

Chapter 6 places the analysis presented in Chapters 2 through 5 into the "real world" of rules review. It presents a case study of JCAR's attempt to revoke through legislative action regulations adopted by the Illinois Department of Nuclear Safety over JCAR's objections. The case study highlights many of the major themes discussed in earlier chapters and underscores the important role that rules review performs as an investigatory and information-gathering process. Finally, Chapter 7 presents a summary of the major analytic generalizations gleaned from Chapters 3 through 6, and offers some concluding observations as to whether rules review is, or can be, an effective means of overseeing the administrative discretion inherent in redelegated rulemaking authority.

2

Rulemaking, Bureaucratic Responsibility, and Constitutional Democracy

THE DILEMMA OF ADMINISTRATIVE DISCRETION

That the presence, continuing growth, and necessity of administrative discretion poses a dilemma for constitutional democracy is part of the "gospel" learned by students of public administration theory. Simply stated, administrative discretion poses a dilemma or paradox for constitutional democracy because it is both problematic and necessary. It is problematic because administrative discretion "conflicts with our fundamental beliefs about institutional limitations and responsibilities" (West 1984, 340–41) and, if left unchecked, it can result in a misconception of the public interest, corruption, or subversion of the bureaucrat's public trust (Rosenbloom 1989, 464–472). Administrative discretion is necessary because of "the complexity and constant evolution of policy needs" that strain the abilities of generalist legislators who do not possess the expertise necessary to confront such changes (West 1984, 342).

Ironically, it is the very actions of the constitutional branches of government, particularly the executive and the legislature, that create the opportunities for administrative discretion, and therefore also the dilemma for constitutional government caused by that discretion. For example, legislatures provide ample opportunities for administrative discretion through both forfeiture and the re-delegation of lawmaking authority to administrative agencies (MacIntyre 1986, 80). Legislatures forfeit administrative discretion to agencies by enacting vague and general laws that fail to clearly circumscribe the details and extent of administrative actions (Shumavon and Hibbeln 1986, 3). The statutory ambiguity in such laws can be attributed to six broad factors that influence lawmaking: (1) the information and time constraints faced by legislatures; (2) the social and economic heterogeneity of the electorate that legislators represent; (3) the difficulties associated with consensus-building within a legislature; (4) the absence of any compelling reasons within a legislature for precisely written statutes; (5) legislative concerns for implementation outcomes; and (6) the fallibility of language (MacIntyre 1986, 69).

Forfeiture is an unconscious act performed by legislatures (Shumavon and Hibbeln 1986, 3). In contrast, redelegation is a conscious legislative action. It deliberately transfers legislative-like discretion to administrative agencies as rulemaking authority. Though traditionally defined in legal-sounding rhetoric, a political definition of redelegation can also be articulated.

> [Re]delegation is better conceptualized as a deliberate abro-
> gation of politically perilous decisions. . . . [I]t is usually
> seen as much more politically expedient to [re]delegate to
> an agency the function of devising rules and regulations that
> restrict behavior of some industry in order to protect some
> segment of the public. . . . [Re]delegation . . . transfers the
> enmity of the regulated industry to the agency. (Shumavon
> and Hibbeln 1986, 3)

In formulating their depiction of redelegation, Shumavon and Hibbeln (1986) engage in at least a bit of hyperbole. Their depiction does underscore that redelegation is a conscious legislative act. But instead of being an "abrogation of politically perilous decisions," redelegation actually takes place along a continuum.

At one end of the continuum, laws bestow rulemaking authority upon administrative agencies for the purpose of "filling in the details" of the law. Rulemaking authority to agencies implementing grant programs, public works, and social security can be placed at this end (Bryner 1987, 7).

At the other end of the continuum are those grants of rulemaking authority that provide almost no guidance as to how this legislative-like discretion is to be exercised. For example, a report prepared by the Illinois House of Representatives Democratic Staff found more than 400 citations where the General Assembly had granted rulemaking authority to administrative agencies. Among these grants of authority, two were particularly broad. The director of the Department of Financial Institutions was authorized to "make and enforce reasonable, relevant regulations, directions, orders, decisions, and findings that may be necessary for the execution of this act" (House Democratic Staff [HDS], Illinois General Assembly 1976, 8). Similarly, the Division of Aeronautics in the Department of Transportation was authorized to "make, promulgate, and amend, change, abrogate, or rescind such reasonable, general, or specific rules, rulings, regulations, and procedures as may be necessary to carry out this act" (HDS 1976, 4).

All points on the continuum bestow some degree of discretion on administrative agencies. But it is rulemaking authority characterized by broad grants of poorly specified discretion that has become the focal point of much public and scholarly criticism. Broad redelegation is accused particularly of producing laws that no longer directly command citizens. Rather, laws are now more likely to be directives and instructions to administrative agencies that command the public through administrative rulemaking (Lowi 1979, 106).

The broad redelegation of legislative-like discretion to administrative agencies allegedly transforms constitutional government by shifting lawmaking and policymaking from legislatures to the bureaucracy. For example, a major impact of broad grants of rulemaking authority is to make administrative agencies the principal source of new laws, rivaling, and in some cases even eclipsing, the lawmaking power constitutionally assigned to legislatures. The growth in rulemaking documented in Chapter 1 clearly illustrates this observation. Relatedly, without close supervision, redelegation encourages the functional independence of administrative agencies from both the legislature and chief executive. Because of this independence, much of the power of government is exercised by unelected bureaucrats not directly accountable to the public. In short, a legislature's redelegation of its lawmaking power to administrative agencies as broad, unspecified rulemaking authority is perceived to conflict with two basic principles of constitutional democracy: (1) representative government; and (2) the separation of powers.

REDELEGATION AND REPRESENTATIVE GOVERNMENT

A central objective of representative government is to secure the accountability of the lawmakers to the governed (Friedrich 1968, 271). One way in which this accountability is secured is through free and open elections in which those who will be governed choose those who will do the actual governing. Under a scheme of representative government, elections substitute consent to be governed for being ruled as the foundation of the state's power. Implicit in this consent is an expectation that those persons or institutions to whom consent is extended will actually exercise the lawmaking authority granted to them. But in redelegating lawmaking authority to administrative agencies, legislatures violate this expectation because they transfer lawmaking authority to unelected administrative agencies, something to which the people had not originally consented.

Through redelegation legislatures lessen the significance of elections as both a means of consent and as a means for those being governed to secure the accountability of those doing the actual governing (Krislov and Rosenbloom 1981, 10–17; Nachmias and Rosenbloom 1980, 30–32). Since the bureaucrats who exercise the redelegated authority are unelected, election can only indirectly influence their behavior. As more lawmaking authority is redelegated to administrative agencies, accountability to the general population declines (Nachmias and Rosenbloom 1980, 32).

Redelegation lessens the significance of elections even further by necessitating a parallel bureaucratization of legislatures to assist in controlling and overseeing the expanded lawmaking authority of administrative agencies. (Krislov and Rosenbloom 1981, 13–14; Nachmias and Rosenbloom 1980, Chapter 5). For example, bureaucratization is now a prominent characteristic in Congress. The bureaucratization of Congress is evident in the extensive use of committee staff and the creation of such congressional agencies as the Congressional Budget Office and the General Accounting Office. This bureaucratization is also increasingly evident among the state legislatures. For example, the Illinois General Assembly has developed a large number of specialized staffs and service agencies to assist it in monitoring the administrative branch (Van Der Slik and Redfield 1986, 95).

The immediate impact of this legislative bureaucratization is a corresponding loss of control over the legislatures by legislators. One way in which this loss is manifested is the transformation of legislatures from deliberative institutions, heavily directed by direct communication among legislators, to institutions where legislative decisions are increasingly based upon staff reports and memorandums (Malbin 1980, 240). To the extent that power within legislatures continues to devolve to legislative bureaucracies, the public's ability to use elections as a means of securing the responsiveness of lawmakers is further eroded (Krislov and Rosenbloom 1981, 14).

REDELEGATION AND SEPARATION OF POWERS

At both the national and state levels of government, separation of powers provides the foundation for the distribution of powers and authority among constitutionally designated governing institutions (Engels 1985). As such, it guards against the undue concentration of governmental power into one branch of government (Freedman 1978; Friedrich 1968; Landis 1938). In its most rigid form, separation of powers is an inflexible doctrine that prohibits any transgression by one branch on the prescribed authority of another branch. Chief Justice Warren Burger's majority opinion in *Immigration and Naturalization Service v. Chadha* (1983) illustrates this rigid interpretation of separation of powers principle:

> The Constitution sought to divide the delegated powers of the new Federal Government into three defined categories ... to assure, as nearly as possible, that each branch of government would confine itself to its assigned responsibilities. The hydraulic pressure inherent within each of the separate Branches to exceed the outer limits of its power, even to accomplish desirable objectives, must be resisted. (462 U.S. 919 at 951)

More recently, in *Bowsher v. Synar* (1986) the Supreme Court declared unconstitutional a key feature of the Gramm-Rudman-Hollings Act, and in doing so advanced an even more rigid model of separation of powers than was in *Chadha* (Fisher 1986, 2). In *Bowsher*, the Court maintained that the Constitution "does not contemplate an active role for Congress in the supervision of officers charged with the execution of the laws it enacts," nor does the "structure of the Constitution ... permit Congress to execute the laws. ... [O]nce Congress makes its choice in enacting legislation, its participation ends. Congress can thereafter control the execution of its enactments only indirectly—by passing new legislation" (54 USLW 5064 at 5066–5069).

Chadha and *Bowsher* inaccurately interpret separation of powers. They do so because the Court's majority gave a "positive reading" to the Constitution, regarding the document as "a set of self-defined terms that require, at most, occasional supplementation from context" (Halton 1989, 128). In reading the Constitution in this way the Court, in both *Chadha* and *Bowsher*, misinterprets separation of powers to such an extent that the Court's majority conflicts with: (1) the intention of the Framers; (2) the general purpose of the principle; (3) precedents; and (4) political necessity (Halton 1989, 131).

Chadha and *Bowsher* depict separation of powers as a wooden, inflexible principle that clearly and definitively defines the powers of each constitutional branch of government. But the Framers "never proposed that the exercise of all of each power be entrusted to one . . . body" (Friedrich 1968, 184). To the contrary, their understanding was flexible and recognized the importance of shared or blended powers among the three branches of government in order to achieve the purposes of separation of powers. This understanding represented a mixture of practical experience with the injustices of state legislatures, the ineptitude of the Continental Congress, and the political theory of Montesquieu (Fisher 1985, 13). These three sources converged in the Framers' conclusion that "[t]here can be no liberty where the legislative and the executive powers are united in the same person, or body of magistrates" (Rossiter 1961, 302).

This conclusion was not intended to completely isolate the power of one branch from that of another branch. As Madison observed in *Federalist 47*, separation did not mean that each branch was "to have no partial agency in or control over the acts of each other" (Rossiter 1961, 302). In fact, Madison, in *Federalist 48*, defended the blending of powers as the best means for preserving the actual principle of separation (Rohr 1986, 19). He noted that "a mere demarcation on parchment" implied by a rigid interpretation of separation of powers was not sufficient to keep the branches separate from each other. Instead, he observed that the principle functioned best when an elaborate series of checks and balances were in place that allowed one branch to exercise in part the powers of another branch, thereby preventing the possible domination of any one branch of government over the other two (Rohr 1986, 19; Rossiter 1961, 313). By preventing such domination, Madison argued that separation of powers also prevented political tyranny: "The accumulation of all powers, legislative, executive, and judiciary, in the same hands, whether of one, a few, or many . . . may justly be pronounced the very definition of tyranny" (Rossiter 1961, 301).

Assuming that Madison faithfully reflected the Framers' intentions regarding separation of powers, they clearly sought to diffuse power across the branches of government to preserve and secure liberty, and a blending of part of those powers was actually necessary to accomplish their goals and to promote a workable government. Separation was to secure liberty and a workable government by inhibiting one branch of government from absorbing the whole power of another branch. As Madison wrote in *Federalist 47*, "Where the whole power of one department is exercised by the same hands which possess the whole power of another, the fundamental principles of a free constitution are subverted" (Rossiter 1961, 302–303). In short, the Framers intended separation to serve multiple purposes. As Justice Robert Jackson observed in *Youngstown Steel Co. v. Sawyer* (1952): "While the Constitution diffuses power to secure liberty, it also contemplates that the practice will integrate the dispersed power into a workable government. It enjoins upon its branches a separateness but interdependence, autonomy but reciprocity" (343 U.S. 579 at 635).

When properly understood, Madisonian separation of powers is clearly not the wooden principle found in *Chadha* and *Bowsher*. Instead, it is a flexible principle that can accommodate the need for redelegation. But this flexibility does not mean that the redelegation of lawmaking power to administrative agencies raises no problems in regard to separation of powers. To understand the proper relationship between redelegation and separation of powers, it is useful to look at a corollary to the principle that states a prohibition on redelegation: *delegata potestas non potest delegari*, which may be translated as meaning that powers delegated to one branch of government through a constitution cannot be redelegated by it to another branch (Pritchett 1984, 184).

Like separation of powers, this corollary principle against redelegation need not be absolutely stated. It, too, is a flexible principle recognizing that in legislating for future events, legislatures confront a true dilemma if forced to rely upon explicit statutory language (Fisher 1985, 102). For example, Chief Justice William Howard Taft observed in *J. W. Hampton, Jr. & Co. v. United States* that the extent and character of permissible redelegation depended upon common sense and the inherent necessities of governmental coordination (Pritchett 1968, 199). Similarly, Chief Justice Charles Evans Hughes wrote in *Schechter Poultry Corp. v. United States* (1935):

> [T]he Constitution has never been regarded as denying to Congress the necessary resources of flexibility and practicality, which will enable it to perform its function in laying down policies and establishing standards, while leaving to select instrumentalities the making of subordinate rules within prescribed limits and the determination of facts to which the policy as declared by the legislature is to apply. (295 U.S. 495 at 530)

Since redelegation has never been categorically forbidden, the real issue surrounding it and separation of powers is unfettered redelegation that would result in a legislature's whole power in a particular area of public policy being absorbed by another branch of government. This conclusion is clearly in keeping with the Framers' original intention discussed earlier. To guard against such absorption, a legislature could stipulate precise statutory standards as to how the administrative agencies are to carry out the redelegated lawmaking power. These standards would reduce the discretion in redelegated authority by defining "the duties and activities . . . in such a detailed way as to make administration [of the redelegated authority] almost a matter of mechanical and compulsory routine" (Landis 1938, 54). But as just previously observed, a major dilemma confronting legislatures is that the future-oriented nature of most legislation inhibits the initial development of precise statutory standards. Statutory precision does not appear to be a realistic means of preventing the potential absorption

of a legislature's whole power that accompanies unfettered redelegation.

Statutory precision can be approximated through a legislature's
reliance upon appropriate oversight techniques designed to promote the responsible exercise of redelegated authority by administrative agencies. Legislative oversight provides a legislature
with opportunities to review administrative exercise of redelegated
authority, and to routinely and regularly revise this authority based
upon the ascertainable administrative experience with it (Lowi
1979, 307). These revisions would presumably narrow the initial
redelegated authority, or more precisely state the authority an
agency actually possessed. In addition, these revisions in redelegated authority prompted by vigorous oversight would lessen
the dilemma between administrative rulemaking and the separation of powers because the exercise of this discretionary authority
would clearly rest upon the juridical principle or, more simply
stated, the rule of law. As one recent commentator observed: "The
rule of law represents the expectations that the exercise of the
coercive powers of government be limited by laws that are clear
and specific, prospective . . . and enforced in a nondiscretionary
manner" (Bryner 1987, 8).

RESPONSIBLE BUREAUCRACY

In the previous section, it was suggested that administrative
rulemaking can be brought within the parameters of constitutional
democracy if this authority is exercised by a responsible bureaucracy. But a precise definition of a responsible bureaucracy is
nearly impossible to state because the term "responsible" is complex and multidimensional. For this reason it is better to think of
bureaucratic responsibility as "a constellation of problems and
procedures for getting the public employee to do well the things
he ought to do, to refrain from doing the things he ought not to do.
It is a pattern of values and ways for realizing them; it is a
governmental house with many procedural mansions" (Powell
1967, 8). For example, it is generally recognized that responsibility
consists of both an internal or subjective component, (e.g., Burke

1986; Finer 1941; Mosher 1982) and an external or objective component (e.g., Boyer 1964; Burke 1986; Friedrich 1968; Krislov and Rosenbloom 1981; Mosher 1982; Powell 1967; Riley 1987; Rosen 1982). Additionally, both the internal and external aspects of responsibility have multiple forms of expression. For example, external responsibility is expressed through administrative responsibility to the general public, interest groups, and the constitutional branches of government (Maass and Radway 1949; Riley 1987; Rosen 1982; Rosenbloom 1983).

External or objective responsibility captures best the relationship among legislative oversight, rulemaking authority, and the more general notion of bureaucratic responsibility. This component of responsibility is akin to the concept of accountability. It concerns itself with the question: Who guards the guardians of the administrative state (Rosenbloom 1989, 463)? External responsibility is built upon the assumption that administrative agencies exercise their discretionary authority irresponsibly; "that, in general, administrative agencies cannot be depended upon to exercise the responsibility necessary to assure that the idea of a government of laws shall prevail" (Boyer 1964, 155). To insure that administrative agencies behave responsibly, it is further assumed that the exercise of administrative discretion must be controlled by holding the agencies themselves accountable to the constitutional branches of government for any misuse of their discretionary authority (Mosher 1982; Spiro 1969).

The goal then of external responsibility is to encourage administrative agencies to develop respect for constitutional principles and the constitutional institutions and processes that grow from the former (Burke 1986, 10–11; Gruber 1987, 23). The successful accomplishment of this goal is important in resolving the dilemma that administrative discretion poses for constitutional democracy because it promotes the legitimacy of administrative exercise of this discretion (Bryner 1987, 78). In this context, legitimacy means "the belief on the part of the population that public administrators have a right . . . to exercise . . . discretion" (Rosenbloom 1989, 443). This legitimacy is important because it "fosters voluntary compliance or obedience to administrative direction and decisions. In its absence, the political community would have to rely on more authoritarian, or highly coercive processes" (Rosenbloom 1989, 443).

LEGISLATIVE OVERSIGHT AND REDELEGATION

The discussion on bureaucratic responsibility helps to reiterate an observation made previously. Legislatures are principal contributors to the growth in administrative discretion and the dilemma that this discretion causes for constitutional democracy (MacIntyre 1986). But the discretionary authority resulting from redelegation need not place a heavy burden upon constitutional democracy if legislatures develop and apply appropriate oversight techniques designed to insure that administrative agencies are held accountable for the responsible exercise of their discretionary authority (Maass and Radway 1949, 186).

A leading and well-respected student of legislative/administrative relations defines legislative oversight as "behavior by legislators and their staffs, individually or collectively, which results in an impact, intended or not, on bureaucratic behavior" (Ogul 1976, 11). This definition underscores an important point. Legislatures possess a wide array of tools and opportunities with which to control and oversee the exercise of administrative discretion. For example, oversight is apparent in such legislative activities as (1) reviewing appropriation requests; (2) investigations; or (3) legislative audits (Jewell and Patterson 1977, Chapter 18; Keefe and Ogul 1981, Chapter 12; Rosen 1982, Chapter 4). It is also evident in such informal activities as casual contacts between legislators and agency officials and constituency casework (Elling 1979). A major shortcoming in these oversight techniques is that they generally do not provide for ongoing and systematic supervision of administrative discretion. They are retrospective in nature and very much like responding to a "fire alarm" rather than being a "police patrol" (McCubbins and Schwartz 1984).

Because of the legislative-like nature of rulemaking authority, traditional oversight techniques must be supplemented with new approaches designed to oversee and control administrative discretion by fostering direct legislative supervision of how administrative agencies exercise their redelegated lawmaking power. The legislative veto and the legislative review of administrative rules, or rules review, are two such techniques. Both require prior legislative approval or review of proposed regulations before the rules can be formally adopted by the issuing agencies. This prospective scrutiny fosters the external responsibility of administrative agencies by allowing the legislature to void or seek revisions in proposed regulations that do not reflect legislative intent or that do not possess proper statutory authority.

The Legislative Veto

In broad terms, a legislative veto is any legislative action that has the effect of cancelling actions taken by either the chief executive or an administrative agency pursuant to existing statutes authorizing those actions (Cooper 1985, 365; Franklin 1986, 492). These legislative actions can be either negative, affirmative, or deliberative procedures (Gilmour 1982, 15–16; Maass 1983, 192–193). In all three instances, a legislature authorizes the chief executive or an administrative agency to develop some plan of action to address a public problem and then requires that plan to be submitted to the legislature for review prior to its implementation. In the negative form, the plan goes into effect after a specific number of days if the legislature has not vetoed it, whereas in the affirmative form, the plan goes into effect only if the legislature takes positive action to approve it either within the whole legislature or its respective committees (Gilmour 1982, 15–16; Maass 1983, 192–193). In the third instance, the plan is submitted to the legislature and goes into effect after a prescribed waiting period unless the legislature passes legislation before the end of the waiting period prohibiting its implementation (Gilmour 1982, 16; Maass 1983, 193).

The manner in which a legislative veto is actually exercised also varies. Affirmative and negative procedures can be exercised by either one or both houses of the legislature, or by the relevant committee of either house of the legislature. Additionally, these vetoes can take the form of a concurrent resolution, one-house resolution, or committee resolution. Neither affirmative nor negative legislative vetoes are presented to the chief executive for his or her approval and are therefore not subject to an executive veto power. In contrast, deliberative procedures promote a law form of the legislative veto wherein the veto action follows the regular legislative process, including both bicameralism and presentment to the chief executive (Cooper 1985, 336–367).

The legislative veto has been used as a legislative tool to control administrative discretion since the 1930s (Harris 1964, 204). It emerged first in Congress as an effort to reconcile two conflicting demands: (1) administrative clamor for broader discretionary authority; and (2) congressional insistence on a way to control this broader discretionary authority that did not depend upon passing any additional laws (Fisher 1985, 162). Within Congress, the legislative veto did not receive wide-scale reliance until the late 1960s; and it was not until 1972 that Congress attached legislative veto provisions to broad grants of redelegated rulemaking authority (Franklin 1986, 494; Sundquist 1981, 344).

Congress has never enacted a legislative veto provision to govern all regulations promulgated by federal administrative agencies (NCSL 1980, 1). The closest Congress has ever come to doing this was in 1976 when two-thirds of the members of the House of Representatives voted in favor of the Administrative Rulemaking Reform Act that would have made all agencies' regulations universally subject to the legislative veto (Fisher 1985, 173; Sundquist 1981, 355). Subsequent efforts to apply the legislative veto to all agency rulemaking were either delayed by the House Judiciary Committee or refused floor action by the House Rules Committee.

Without congressional action, it has generally been the state legislatures that have developed the legislative veto as a means by which to secure the accountability of administrative rulemaking.

Indeed, the legislative veto may be "the most far-reaching step taken by [state] legislatures to redress their loss of control ... over rulemaking" (Johnson 1983, 99). Within the state legislatures, the legislative veto has undergone certain changes. It is often one component of a more encompassing rules review process. The legislative veto is also normally a multistep process beginning with the suspension of a proposed regulation by the rules review committee and then requiring that suspension to be sustained by the full legislature.

The legislative veto provides legislatures with a potentially effective means of overseeing agency implementation of their rulemaking authority. But both federal and state courts have severely limited its use. At the federal level, the United States Supreme Court struck down congressional use of the legislative veto in *Immigration and Naturalization Service v. Chadha* (1983). A majority of the justices concluded that the legislative veto violated the presentment clause of Article I because the resolution used to invoke the veto was not presented to the president for his signature. A legislative veto implemented by a one-house resolution was additionally unconstitutional because it violated the bicameral provision of the Constitution. The legislative veto was also perceived to be unconstitutional because it violated the principle of separation of powers by allowing Congress to intrude too far into executive branch activities. By striking down the legislative veto, the Court's majority was telling Congress that it "must abide by its delegation of authority until that delegation is legislatively altered or revoked" (462 U.S. 919 at 955).

The legislative veto has not fared any better among the various state courts that have ruled upon it. In all state cases where its constitutionality has been questioned, the court decisions have gone against the legislative veto (Johnson 1983, 100–101). For example, two years prior to Chadha the Alaska Supreme Court struck down the legislative veto in its state because the legislative veto violated the presentment clause of the Alaska Constitution. It was additionally struck down because it violated the legislative enactment provisions of the state's constitution (Johnson 1983, 100).

Judicial pronouncements on the constitutionality of the legislative veto appear to undermine its use in controlling and overseeing administrative rulemaking. But contrary to the initial impressions, these judicial rulings have not completely crippled the legislative veto or thoroughly removed it from a legislature's oversight arsenal. For example, within one year after *Chadha*, Congress had enacted nearly two dozen veto provisions in the congressional form (Cooper 1985, 385). A principal reason for the continued survival of the legislative veto is the generally flawed logic of the judicial decisions challenging its constitutionality (Cooper 1983, 1985; Franklin 1986).

Writing specifically about *Chadha*, but equally applicable to state court decisions, Cooper (1985, 370) argues that in distinguishing between legislative, executive, or administrative power, courts have applied the wrong criterion. The Supreme Court, other federal courts, and state courts have emphasized the stages of decision making. This in turn is buttressed by a "formalistic separation of powers analysis in which [courts have] simply defined all administrative activities as executive" (West and Cooper 1989, 24). Because of their rigid, formalistic analysis of separation of powers, judicial decisions like *Chadha* are easy to characterize as "bull-in-the-china-shop" decisions that may reach the right result for one party in the case, but are nevertheless completely incorrect in their rationale (De Seife 1984, 306).

In contrast, a functional analysis of the separation of powers principle supports the constitutionality of a legislative veto of administrative rulemaking (Cooper 1985; West and Cooper 1989). In a functional analysis, administration is recognized as combining all three essential functions of government and special attention is paid to the substance and content of administrative authority. One purpose of a functional analysis is to allow courts to allocate oversight responsibilities for administration among the constitutional branches of government in such a way as to maintain and promote an institutional balance (West and Cooper 1989, 24). In a functional analysis, the legislative-like quality of rulemaking can justify direct legislative influence and control over it, whereas the more adjudicative aspects of administration would not be susceptible to legislative control.

Justice Lewis Powell gave practical expression to a functional analysis of the separation of powers and administration in his concurring opinion in *Chadha*:

> Functionally, the doctrine may be violated in two ways. One branch may interfere . . . with the other's performance of its constitutionally assigned functions. . . . Alternatively, the doctrine may be violated when one branch assumes a function that more properly is entrusted to another. (462 U.S. 919 at 963)

Applying these functional standards, Justice Powell proceeded to examine the action of the Immigration and Naturalization Service granting Chadha a permanent residence status and found it to be adjudicative in nature. Turning next to the legislative veto that set aside the decision of the Immigration and Naturalization Service, Justice Powell concluded "[w]hen Congress finds that a particular person does not satisfy the statutory criteria for permanent residence in this country it has assumed a judicial function in violation of the principle of separation of powers" (462 U.S. 919 at 960).

Even if future courts reject functional analysis of separation of powers and administration, the legislative veto remains an attractive means by which to oversee rulemaking because of its several forms. As noted earlier, the legislative veto comes in either a legislative form that is not presented to a chief executive, or a law form that is presented. Cases such as *Chadha* have ruled only on the constitutionality of the first type of legislative veto. Based upon the reasoning in *Chadha*, the law form is clearly constitutional and can therefore be relied upon to oversee administrative rulemaking. In particular, Cooper (1985, 384) suggests that for rulemaking, joint resolutions of negation are the preferred mode of the law form veto because regulations "are too important to be left to waiting period control and too numerous to be subjected to individual approval."

Rules Review

As defined in Chapter 1, the legislative review of administrative rulemaking or rules review is a state-level oversight process that currently has no direct equivalent at the congressional level. As prescribed by statute, rules review is usually part of a state's administrative procedure act requiring all state agencies to submit all proposed regulations to a specially designated committee for its prior review or its prior approval before the regulations are formally adopted and implemented by the issuing agency. The principal function usually assigned to a rules review process is to insure that proposed regulations are within statutory authority and reflect legislative intent.

Rules review is ongoing and generally affects all regulations. For this reason, it may be considered as a more systematic approach to overseeing administrative rulemaking than the legislative veto. Indeed, as state experience with both techniques suggests, rules review may be a necessary first step toward an effective use of the legislative veto. Rules review allows for the necessary legislative investigation and analysis of regulations to occur for the purpose of determining whether or not reliance upon the legislative veto is necessary to correct discovered administrative abuses.

Rules review has existed in some state legislatures since the early 1940s. For example, the Michigan state legislature has relied upon rules review since 1943 (Schubert 1958, 138). But in most state legislatures, rules review has existed only since the late 1960s to the late 1970s. The specific experiences that have led the state legislatures to adopt rules review vary, but the common denominators among their experiences have been the growth in redelegated lawmaking authority, the corresponding increase in administrative rulemaking, and the real or perceived administrative abuses resulting from uncontrolled redelegation. For example, the Maryland legislature adopted rules review because of its increased concern about the rules and regulations promulgated by Maryland agencies and legislative interest in "reaffirming its prerogative of legislative oversight" (Legislative Study Group [LSG], Maryland General Assembly 1977, 1). The Pennsylvania General Assembly adopted rules review as "more individuals, organizations, and businesses began to realize that the formulation of and implementation of regulations often affected them more directly than did the development and passage of legislation" (State Government Committee [SGC], Pennsylvania General Assembly 1986, 5).

Forty-two state legislatures now rely upon rules review to make administrative rulemaking accountable. The actual process among these state legislatures varies with regard to (1) structure; (2) the scope of the review; (3) the powers of the reviewing committee; and (4) the staff resources committed to it (NCSL 1979). For example, in the Wisconsin state legislature, rules review is conducted in combination with the standing committees in both houses and a special joint committee (Berger 1983, 103). In Pennsylvania, rules review is conducted by an independent commission comprised of nonlegislators, four chosen by the legislature and one chosen by the governor (Proffer 1984, 24). In most states, rules review is conducted by a joint committee (31 states) with the authority to review all proposed regulations (37 states) and pre-existing regulations (33 states) (Council of State Governments [CSG] 1987, 131).

In most state legislatures, the role of these rules review committees is principally advisory. As of 1988, 14 reviewing committees were additionally empowered to suspend proposed regulations under extreme circumstances (CSG 1989, 133). For example, in Illinois, the state's administrative procedure act authorizes JCAR to suspend a proposed regulation for 180 days if the Committee determines that the rule poses a serious threat to the public interest, safety, or welfare. (IAPA, Section 7.07a).

Concluding Caveats

Both the legislative veto and rules review have been presented as means of overseeing administrative rulemaking authority resulting from redelegation. Both implicitly and explicitly, these two oversight techniques have also been presented as ways in which the constitutional dilemma surrounding administrative discretion can be, at least, partially resolved. But it would be naive to assert only the virtues of the legislative veto and rules review and to ignore their possible shortcomings.

In their ideal form, both the legislative veto and rules review are institutional tools designed to promote the institutional integrity of Congress and the state legislatures by securing the accountability of administrative agencies to the rule of law. But as one recent commentator observed, much of the effort to limit bureaucratic discretion can be harnessed for narrow political interest while "couched in the rhetoric of political accountability and the rule of law" (Bryner 1987, 8). For example, critics of the legislative veto maintain that, at least within Congress, veto reviews are used largely by members of Congress in response to constituent complaints rather than to insure that regulations are within statutory authority and reflective of legislative intent. Relatedly, the legislative veto in Congress is perceived to increase the power of committees and subcommittees rather than the Congress as a whole, thereby undermining its institutional integrity (Gilmour 1982, 18–20). Similarly, available data suggest that state legislators who serve on a rules review committee may also show little hesitation in promoting their own interests and definition of legislative intent over those of the state legislatures (Ethridge 1985, 29).

If rules review or the legislative veto is used to enhance the power of individual legislators, or to substitute their intent for the intent of a legislature as a whole, the oversight conducted through either of these processes will be as constitutionally disturbing as if the redelegated lawmaking power remained unaccountable. This is because the advancement of the individual legislators would be at the expense of the legislature as a whole. Additionally, these legislators would, in effect, be acquiring lawmaking power that properly belonged to the institution.

While both the legislative veto and rules review represent a potential threat to legislatures as a whole, this threat should not be overstated. For example, the threat posed by the legislative veto is greatly reduced by relying upon law forms requiring approval by both houses of a legislature. The threat posed by rules review is similarly reduced by its general advisory nature. Because of this restriction on their authority, the rules review committees in most states lack the means to routinely substitute their intent for the intent of their respective state legislatures. The advisory nature of their power means that these committees will function primarily as a routinized investigatory body gathering information on potential abuses in the agencies' exercise of their redelegated lawmaking powers.

3

Establishing Rules Review in a State Legislature

INTRODUCTION

Why is a state legislature likely to establish a rules review process? The Illinois experience suggests at least two possible explanations: (1) a legislature wishes to reclaim lawmaking authority lost through redelegation; or (2) it wishes to provide to the affected publics relief from overburdensome regulations. The Illinois experience further suggests that both of these legislative motivations for establishing rules review are likely to evolve from a more general legislative perception of a runaway and unaccountable state bureaucracy.

A RUNAWAY BUREAUCRACY

Due in large part to its own propensity toward redelegation dating back to at least 1874, the Illinois General Assembly was confronted in the middle 1970s by what its members perceived to be a runaway and unaccountable state bureaucracy. Redelegation was so widespread that a 1976 report prepared by the Illinois Legislative Council listed 403 specific grants of rulemaking authority to administrative agencies. Typically, the rulemaking authority granted to these agencies was quite broad. For example, the Meat and Poultry Inspection Act simply stated: "The Director of Agriculture shall make rules and regulations necessary to administer the . . . Act" (Legislative Council [LC], Illinois General Assembly 1976, 6). These broad grants of rulemaking authority were accompanied by few specific legislative guidelines as to how the authority was to be exercised. Typical of the procedural requirements were those accompanying the rulemaking authority of the Illinois Department of Labor. Labor could promulgate "rules only after proper notice ha[d] been given" (HDS 1976, 9). No other procedures were required and what constituted proper notice was not elaborated.

Broad grants of a rulemaking authority with few specific procedural guidelines created an impression within the General Assembly of a runaway and unaccountable state bureaucracy issuing regulations made in an arbitrary and capricious manner with total disregard for legislative intent. State legislators' perceptions of a runaway bureaucracy were further intensified by business opposition to the environmental regulations issued by the Illinois Pollution Control Board. A representative for one of Illinois' leading business associations noted that the business community was seeking relief from the social and environmental regulations that imposed undue economic burden on them. The business community felt that establishing legal procedures for rulemaking and some form of oversight would, in part, provide the regulatory relief they sought.

In some ways the impression held by members of the General Assembly and the business community was correct. By the middle 1970s Illinois state agencies had promulgated over 300 volumes of regulations, many of which had been clearly adopted in a haphazard and unsystematic manner. For example, rulemaking at the Illinois Department of Children and Family Services was quite disorganized. Rulemaking was what one employee called a "loose process." What Children and Family Services (CFS) did might not actually be called rulemaking in that the department relied upon office memos to field personnel stating what CFS's policy would be in any given area. Each unit acted on its own, and little coordination or consensus building across units was sought. In addition, public comment was seldom, if ever, solicited.

Additionally, numerous regulations appeared to be not carefully thought out and just plain ridiculous. An October 29, 1980 guest editorial in the *Chicago Tribune* by Sen. Prescott Bloom details several illustrations: (1) a set of regulations promulgated by the Illinois Commerce Commission imposing a 101-page accounting system on small businesses that towed trespassing vehicles; (2) a Department of Conservation rule requiring that all metal grills used in state parks be approved by the park rangers; (3) a regulation promulgated by the Illinois Liquor Control Commission including commercial airlines in its definition of railroads; and (4) a Department of Corrections regulation allowing inmates to go on family outings with volunteer groups, but the outings were "not to be used for the purpose of family visits."

RECLAIMING LAWMAKING POWER

The Illinois General Assembly responded in 1976–77 to the seemingly runaway and unaccountable state bureaucracy by establishing a rules review process and JCAR charged with its implementation. Both rules review and JCAR were the second stage of a more general legislative effort that began in 1975, and continues through today, designed to standardize administrative procedures and control the exercise of administrative discretion. In establishing its new rules review process, the General Assembly was reacting to the two principal perceived effects of unrestrained rulemaking: (1) the continued erosion of the preeminence of legislative lawmaking; and (2) the imposition of overburdensome regulations on the regulated publics, particularly the business community. Through rules review, the General Assembly hoped to counteract both these existing conditions by reclaiming for itself lost lawmaking power and providing regulatory relief to affected publics.

The General Assembly's motivation to use rules review and JCAR to reestablish its lawmaking dominance over state government was clearly evident in the House and Senate debates on the legislation proposed throughout the latter 1970s and early 1980s that created and refined both the process and the Joint Committee. For example, in a statement before the House Executive Committee, Rep. Harry "Buzz" Yourell of Oak Lawn, the sponsor of House Bill 14 creating rules review and JCAR, stated that the new process "would increase our input into administrative rulemaking. Administrative rules have the full force of law and it is time we assert our constitutional authority as the law-making body of government" (Yourell 1976, 2). During the House floor debates on House Bill 14, Representative Yourell carried forward this same theme:

> House Bill 14 . . . would go a long way toward insuring responsible legislative oversight of the rulemaking functions of state agencies. In many instances, administrative rules are more significant than enabling legislation that authorizes them. Yet there does not appear presently to be a workable way for the Legislature to maintain oversight, let alone control, for this increasingly important government function. (May 4, 1977, 20)

In 1979 Representative Yourell, who was then secretary of JCAR, once again underscored the need for the General Assembly to exert more control over administrative rulemaking. Speaking in support of legislation that sought to have state agencies bear the burden of proof in any court challenge against regulations adopted over JCAR's objections, he observed:

> Senate Bill 307 is an important piece of legislation that will give to the Joint Committee on Administrative Rules an additional tool for dealing with agency rules which violate or ignore the statutory authority of the agency. . . . [I]t also gives to the Legislature an effective means of dealing with agency rules which completely ignore our legislative enactment. It helps restore to us, the elected Representatives of the people, control over the law which agency bureaucrats are making. (Senate Bill 307, June 18, 1979, 115)

The principal arguments for incorporating a legislative veto into the rules review process also showed the General Assembly's desire to reclaim the lawmaking authority it had lost through redelegation. For example, Rep. Cal Skinner of Crystal Lake noted that what the legislative veto "tries to do is give us, as members of the General Assembly, an ability to undo the horrible things that the Executive Branch does with . . . the bills we pass. You will see bills that you have written come out with regulations you cannot believe . . . yet you have no remedy whatsoever except to change the law" (House Bill 1503, April 15, 1980, 33).

The Illinois General Assembly created rules review and JCAR, in part, to reclaim lawmaking power lost through redelegated rulemaking authority. For those legislators who serve on JCAR this goal of reclaiming and now maintaining the preeminence of the General Assembly's lawmaking power remains a principal goal. They see rules review accomplishing this goal by "placing the General Assembly back into the implementation of administrative rulemaking" and making JCAR the "eyes, ears and voice of the General Assembly when it comes to regulations."* In maintaining the General Assembly's lawmaking powers vis-à-vis the administrative branch of state government, these JCAR legislators also voice an appreciation for the impact of their actions on constitutional government. The combined thoughts of two JCAR legislators particularly reveal this understanding: "Without some form of rules review, unelected officials would be erroneously interpreting legislative intent" [and] "if the bureaucracy was to take over, representative government as we know it is over."

PROVIDING REGULATORY RELIEF

As previously observed, a state legislature may also create a rules review process to provide some degree of regulatory relief to the affected publics. But care should be taken not to draw too major

---

*All unreferenced quotes are taken from confidential interviews conducted by the author with past and present participants in the Illinois rules review process. For additional information on these interviews see the methodological essay in the Appendix.

a distinction between the goal of providing regulatory relief and reclaiming lost lawmaking power. As the following discussion makes clear, for the Illinois General Assembly, and probably for most other state legislatures, the two objectives for rules review are likely to be intertwined. Reclaiming lost lawmaking power by assuring that regulations are faithful to legislative intent and premised upon statutory authority will, in effect, lessen the regulatory burden that administrative agencies seek to impose upon the affected publics.

Like its goal to reclaim lost lawmaking power, the Illinois General Assembly's interest in regulatory relief is also revealed in the House and Senate debates on legislation proposed to refine rules review and JCAR. For example, in 1979 during debate on the proposed legislation to reverse the burden of proof, Rep. Donald Deuster of Mundelein noted: "If there's anything we should do on behalf of the individual citizens and business enterprises in the State of Illinois, we should take every possible step to limit and curtail Executive Branch excesses and over-regulation" (Senate Bill 307, November 1, 1979, 116). Rep. Ronald Stearney of Chicago also argued that this new authority should be added to the existing rules review process in order to insure that the affected publics received relief from overburdensome regulations: "They say the vested interests are for this. Absolutely, because those faceless bureaucrats have restrained them and put a great burden on their shoulders over the years. And there is no way to attack them" (Senate Bill 307, November 1, 1979, 160).

Members of the General Assembly also viewed the addition of a legislative veto to rules review as a tool by which to lessen the burden of over-regulating the affected publics. For example, Rep. Jack Davis of Chicago observed that the legislative veto was necessary to "insure the slowing down of the proliferation of bad regulations in State Government" (House Bill 1503, June 27, 1980, 165). Senator Arthur Berman of Chicago, who was a member of JCAR, noted: "Our constituents are looking for help out of the burdensome regulations that are imposed upon them. This will help our constituents" (House Bill 1503, December 3, 1980, 29). Similarly, Senator Bloom observed that the legislative veto "would cut down on the unwarranted and excessive intrusion of the bureaucracy in our day-to-day affairs" (House Bill 1503, December 3, 1980, 29). Finally, Rep. George Hudson of Hinsdale commented: "Our people . . . are suffering from . . . rules and regulations that have the effect of laws that are not, in effect, made by the Representatives of the people" (House Bill 1503, April 15, 1980, 39).

The House and Senate debates on the legislative veto and the attempt to reverse the burden of proof illustrate the Illinois General Assembly's interest in promoting regulatory relief. Other less controversial amendments to the IAPA sponsored by JCAR also show that the Committee and the General Assembly sought to use rules review to advance regulatory relief. For example, JCAR believed that "small businesses [were] unduly burdened by the rules and regulations promulgated by various state agencies" (JCAR 1982, 22). To promote regulatory relief to small businesses, JCAR, in 1981, sponsored the Regulatory Flexibility Act, legislation principally developed by the Illinois State Chamber of Commerce and small business organizations (JCAR 1982, 22). The proposed act required state agencies to (1) consider different methods for reducing the impact of their regulations on small businesses; (2) solicit and consider the public comments of small businesses that are likely to be affected by the agencies' regulations; and (3) file two regulatory flexibility analyses on how proposed regulations are likely to affect small businesses (JCAR 1982, 22).

A second area where JCAR stressed regulatory relief was in the exercise of discretionary authority. From the earliest day of its review, JCAR objected to proposed regulations because they lacked specific standards by which the agencies would exercise their discretionary authority. Though JCAR believed that it possessed the implicit authority to require agencies to provide standards, the Committee sought to incorporate this apparent legal requirement into the IAPA (JCAR 1980, 120). This was accomplished in 1979 when the General Assembly passed Senate Bill 419, requiring that "[e]ach rule that implements a discretionary power to be exercised by an agency . . . include the standards by which the agency shall exercise the power" (JCAR 1980, 120).

A third area of regulatory relief closely akin to precise standards that JCAR pursued for the General Assembly was to make all regulations both readable and understandable to the general public. Through its review of existing regulations, JCAR concluded that a large number of the regulations it was reviewing could not be understood by persons with a high-school education or less. To correct this situation, JCAR sponsored House Bill 834. This proposed amendment to the IAPA required "all state agencies' rules to be written in clear and plain English" (JCAR 1981, 128). Clear and plain English was defined as (1) simple words used in their commonly understood meanings and conveying meanings clearly and directly; (2) positive statements written in the present tense; (3) simple sentences that are short rather than compound or complex; (4) the exclusion of unnecessary definitions; and (5) language that presents the regulation in a clear and coherent manner (JCAR 1981, 144).

In one of the more ironic events in the development of rules review in Illinois, House Bill 834 had to be amended because, as it was introduced into the General Assembly, the Plain English Bill was not in plain and clear English. Even after it was amended, some legislators still complained that House Bill 834 was not well written. During the House debate on the bill, Rep. Richard Brummer of Effingham commented to Rep. Richard Kelly of Hazel Crest, who was a member of JCAR and the sponsor of the bill: "Representative Kelly, I think this an admirable idea. I have the Bill in front of me, and the problem is I can't understand the Bill. I don't know if it's written in plain and clear English" (House Bill 834, March 24, 1982, 31).

EXTERNAL AND INTERNAL PARITY

Rules review was widely adopted by state legislatures during the 1970s—a decade marked by a large number of legislative reforms and improvements designed to enable state legislatures to assert more aggressively their authority over the administrative branch of government (Rosenthal 1981a, 124). The basic motivation behind reforms like rules review was a legislative desire to reestablish a balance of power or parity between state legislatures and the executive/administrative branch of state government. The Illinois General Assembly's creation of JCAR reflected this basic motivation. In a 1982 article, Sen. Prescott Bloom, a principal architect of rules review in Illinois, observed:

> The branches of government need to be balanced. . . . In Illinois the massive increase in the executive branch's power and the parallel growth of administrative agencies has reduced the legislative branch to a poor cousin, instead of an equal partner. The legislature is simply unable to effectively check the actions of the executive. . . . Review and veto of administrative rules is one mechanism that the legislature has found to restore parity with the executive branch of government. (Bloom 1982, 33)

The creation of rules review and other legislative reforms in the 1970s characterized "just what an independent and assertive legislature [was] suppose[d] to do": check the growth of administrative power and maintain its own constitutional authority as the principal lawmaking body in state government (Rosenthal 1981a, 124). Legislative reforms designed to reassert control over administrative discretion underscored an awareness among at least some state legislators of the legal and institutional position of a legislature within constitutional government and the necessity of maintaining its institutional integrity vis-à-vis the other branches of government. Rules review, in particular, was a further recognition that legislation is the primary instrument of power for a state legislature and any uncontrolled or non-overseen encroachment of that power results in a parallel loss of prestige and authority for the whole legislature.

This sensitivity to its place vis-à-vis the other branches of state government suggests a partial explanation for the type of rules review process implemented in most states. In creating new institutional processes like rules review, state legislatures, in the 1970s, were sensitive to the potential erosion of their lawmaking power from any quarter. They were concerned with both external parity among the different branches of government and internal parity between the legislature as a whole and its subdivisions. JCAR's early history illustrates this legislative concern for internal parity.

The potential threat that JCAR and rules review posed to the lawmaking power of the General Assembly as a whole was clearly a concern of some legislators, and justifiably so. From the natural arrogance accompanying any new organization, JCAR, early in its existence, sought substantive expansion of its power over administrative rulemaking that, if abused, would have resulted in the Committee absorbing much of the lawmaking power of the General Assembly. Ironically, JCAR pursued these reforms principally because the advisory nature of its review forced it to rely upon the general lawmaking power of the General Assembly to secure agency compliance with its review of proposed regulations.

To secure compliance from unresponsive agencies, JCAR's principal recourse was to introduce corrective legislation into the General Assembly. The Committee concluded that this necessity seriously limited its control over administrative rulemaking. Any corrective measures it sought to take involved "a long process of consideration by the General Assembly during which time the presumption is in favor of the agency since the rule is allowed to be effective and enforced, regardless of the seriousness or strength of legislative opposition" (JCAR 1980, 392). To correct this perceived deficiency, Senator Bloom instructed the Committee's staff to prepare a position paper on alternatives to corrective legislation.

In its report, the Committee's staff proposed a number of alternatives. First, it suggested that all proposed rules be required to have the Committee's approval before they could take effect. This alternative sought to transform the Committee's authority from advisory review to binding. Second, JCAR's staff suggested that the Committee seek the authority to initiate court action on behalf of the people of Illinois against agencies that failed to comply with committee objections. Third, JCAR's staff suggested that the

Committee seek legislation that would require the agencies to bear the burden of proof in any court challenge to regulations adopted over JCAR's objections.

The alternatives proposed by JCAR's staff revealed to whom it believed the state agencies were accountable and how the Committee perceived its relationship with the General Assembly. All three alternatives excluded the full legislature from participating in the accountability sought from the state agencies. Each alternative sought to make the state agencies accountable first to JCAR. JCAR would be authorized to initiate court action; JCAR's objections would be the basis for reversing the burden of proof; and JCAR's prior approval of regulations would be necessary before their final adoption. These alternatives also provided no assurance that JCAR's own activities were in any way accountable to the General Assembly. None of the alternatives provided a check by the General Assembly on JCAR's behavior.

JCAR's arrogance toward the General Assembly did not go unnoticed, as a highly visible and vocal group of legislators cautioned against JCAR's attempt to encroach upon the lawmaking powers of the full Assembly. For example, Rep. Harry Leinenweber of Joliet described the 1979 JCAR-sponsored burden of proof legislation as "another power-grab by a committee seeking more and more power to the extent that [it] may become the actual legislative body of this state and we would be advisory to the Joint Committee" (Senate Bill 307, June 18, 1979, 117–118). Rep. Sam Vinson of Clinton echoed Representative Leinenweber's sentiments by observing that the burden of proof legislation would allow JCAR "to substitute [its] willful judgment for this Legislature and you can trust that willful judgment through time will be eventually abused" (Senate Bill 307, November 1, 1979, 159–160).

Speaking in opposition to a JCAR-sponsored bill authorizing a legislative veto, Rep. Phillip Collins of Chicago pointed toward the visible signs of the Committee's growing power:

> Now I think that this Administrative Committee is one of the finest things we have created but I'm fearful over the

growth of this Committee and the power it yields and
wishes to yield. . . . I don't know how many of you have
gone across the street and looked at their quarters in the
Lincoln Tower. . . . They've taken over the entire caucus
room . . . for office space and they're continually hiring
additional people. I think this is an empire that has to have
the reins put upon it rapidly. (House Bill 1503, April 15,
1980, 41)

Perhaps Representative Vinson summed up best why legislators
were reluctant to move beyond an advisory review process:

The problem . . . is that . . . one Committee, one small
group of the Legislature . . . takes the authority from the
full Legislature so that when a Member of this House votes
on a Bill, sponsors a Bill, passes a Bill . . . , a small group
of this House and of the Senate can come back and defeat
that total intent. . . . The problem with this Bill . . . is that
the individual Members may take some authority away
from the existing bureaucracy while they vest it in a new
bureaucracy, the Joint Committee. (Senate Bill 1822, June
25, 1980, 31)

In brief, state legislatures are likely to resist efforts to establish
anything other than advisory review because of the potential
internal threat to the legislature posed by binding review. In
particular, the overly broad delegation of a legislature's oversight
power to a specialized committee creates the potential for the will
of a few legislators to be substituted for the whole, and for
lawmaking power to be transferred merely from an old bureaucracy to a new legislative bureaucracy. But as will be discussed in
Chapter 5, the absence of binding review is likely to decrease the
probability that agencies will be responsive to the accountability
sought through rules review. In securing internal parity between
the oversight committee and the legislature as a whole, a state
legislature may find its ability to achieve external parity with state
agencies lessened.

4

The Nature of Rules Review

INTRODUCTION

A state legislature may incorporate rules review into its oversight arsenal to reclaim lost lawmaking power and provide regulatory relief to the affected publics. But once incorporated, an important question needs to be explored. What is the nature of the rules review process that is implemented? The nature of a rules review process reveals for what state agencies are being held accountable and to whom they are actually accountable.

Admittedly, the nature of rules review is likely to vary among the state legislatures employing it (Ethridge 1985). But as the following discussion illustrates, the Illinois experience with rules review does suggest some aspects of the nature of rules review that are likely to be found in other state legislatures. For example, that there should be a congruity between the accountability sought from state agencies by a rules review process and the reasons why a state legislature adopted it is one logical assumption that grows out of the Illinois experience. The Illinois experience also suggests two important basic characteristics of rules review that are likely to influence the accountability sought from state agencies and to whom they are actually accountable: (1) legislators' perceptions of the relevance of rules review to other aspects of legislative life;

and (2) the influence of legislative staff on the implementation of rules review.

THE NATURE OF RULES REVIEW IN ILLINOIS

In Illinois, rules review is the product of both legislative staff and committee review of proposed regulations. But both JCAR legislators and former JCAR staff persons agree that the committee's staff dominates the review process. For example, former JCAR staff persons estimate that as much as 75 to 95 percent of all rules review is initiated and resolved at the staff level. The nature of this staff review, and therefore the accountability sought from it, is detailed in the questions regarding proposed regulations that JCAR's staff asks the state agencies. Table 1 describes this substance by presenting the five principal types of staff questions presented to the state agencies.

Table 1
Leading Types of Staff Questions

Type	N	%
Rules Reflect Policies / Procedures of Department	594	34
Regulatory Clarity	433	24
Standards for the Exercise of Discretionary Authority	234	13
Statutory Authority and Legislative Intent	96	5

Note: For a discussion of the data used to create Table 1 see the Appendix.

A plurality of 34 percent of all staff questions are concerned with whether proposed regulations accurately reflect the policies and procedures of the issuing agencies. These questions solicit further explanations from the state agencies as to why they are proceeding with a particular course of action. Former JCAR staff persons note that these questions are, in effect, "fishing expeditions" designed to find additional shortcomings in the regulations. A typical example of a policies and procedures question is found in the Department of Children and Family Services' regulation concerning the placement of a child with foster parents who are related to him or her. In this regulation, the Department stipulated that a female child could not share a bedroom with an adult male. The staff attorney conducting the review sought further clarification of the Department's policy by asking why such a gender-based classification was in the regulation.

The second principal type of staff question concerns the regulatory clarity of proposed regulations. These questions, 25 percent of the total, are directed primarily toward vague and unclear wording of regulations and definitions of terminology and phraseology. Typical of this type of question is the staff review of the Illinois Department of Registration and Education's regulation implementing the Illinois Public Accounting Act. In this regulation, the Department had designated a "recognized educational or professional sponsor" of continuing education courses to be a college or university "approved by the appropriate governing board, or equivalent public authority . . . to grant degrees" (Johnson 1985). The JCAR staff person responsible for the review of this regulation asked Registration and Education to define the phrases "appropriate governing board" and "equivalent public authority" (Johnson 1985).

The third type of question concerns the standards by which agencies exercise their discretionary authority. These questions account for 13 percent of the total questions asked. Standards questions are designed principally to reduce the potential arbitrariness of administrative behavior by placing within the regulations the criteria that the agencies will consider when exercising discretionary decision-making authority. The Illinois Department of Children and Family Services' regulation entitled Relative Home Placement provides a good illustration of standards questions.

The Department's regulation on relative home placement was proposed to insure that foster parents who were related to children for whom the Department was legally responsible met the same criteria as nonrelated foster parents. In proposing this regulation, the Department intentionally did not specify how its field personnel responsible for enforcing the regulation would determine if the foster parents had failed to adequately care for the foster child. The Department sought to allow the supervising personnel the maximum amount of discretionary authority necessary to respond to the needs of the foster child.

This broad use of discretion apparently unleashed in the JCAR staff person responsible for the review fears of the Department's personnel behaving arbitrarily and capriciously with the relative foster parents. In his review, he asked the Department 42 questions regarding the standards by which the supervising personnel would exercise their discretionary authority. For example, the staff attorney sought greater specification of the standards that would be used to determine such things as whether or not (1) the foster child's meals were balanced; (2) a household pet posed a danger to the child; (3) the foster child's bedroom was comfortable and suitably furnished for the child's age and sex; and (4) the health, safety, and welfare of the foster child was endangered.

Drafting and editing questions are the fourth most common type of question staff members ask the state agencies. These questions represent another 13 percent of all questions asked. Drafting and editing questions focus on the agencies' use of proper grammar, punctuation, and spelling. The presence of these questions suggests that JCAR's staff spends a substantial amount of its time copyediting for the state agencies. For example, of the 55 drafting and editing questions a JCAR staff person raised regarding a proposed Illinois Department of Registration and Education regulation, 54 percent of them were concerned with the insertion and deletion of commas.

Statutory Authority Questions

In contrast to the first four types of questions, very few staff questions appear to be directed at the legal authority of proposed regulations. As Table 1 reports, only 5 percent of the questions raised by JCAR's rules analysts and staff attorneys concern the statutory authority or legislative intent of proposed regulations. Because the sample of staff questions was biased toward major rulemaking, in which statutory authority questions were likely to occur, this percentage may actually be inflated. The statutory authority questions rarely challenge the overt authority of the state agencies to promulgate their regulations. Instead, staff review is directed at prohibiting the state agencies from using implicit statutory authority as justification for provisions within their regulations that were not explicitly authorized by the legislature. A good example of JCAR treatment of implicit statutory authority is the staff review of the Illinois Department of Commerce and Community Affairs' regulation implementing a grant program for local tourism and convention bureaus.

In 1984, the Illinois General Assembly authorized the Department of Commerce and Community Affairs to distribute grants to local tourism and convention bureaus for the purpose of promoting local tourism in Illinois. The General Assembly was silent as to the details of how the program was to be implemented. In establishing the regulation to govern the program, the Department of Commerce and Community Affairs adopted a rule that faithfully implemented the general intent of the General Assembly. But in doing so, the Department relied upon implicit rulemaking authority to insure the cost effectiveness of the program and that the allocated funds were not misappropriated. In particular, local tourism and convention bureaus receiving grant money under the program would have to be audited by the Department. Ten percent of the appropriated funds were also set aside to conduct these audits. In addition, the Department required that the local tourism and convention bureaus provide dollar-for-dollar matching funds, display the Department's logo on all promotional materials printed and distributed, and denied future eligibility to local bureaus found to misuse program funds.

On each of the above provisions, the JCAR staff person conducting the review questioned the Department's use of implicit statutory authority. These questions were raised despite the fact that the Department of Commerce and Community Affairs had followed the general intent of the General Assembly and had incorporated these additional provisions to insure the success of the grant program. Unable to resolve these questions, the staff person recommended that the Committee object to the proposed regulations because "the Department lacks the statutory authority to implement program, administrative, and application requirements on local tourism and convention bureaus" (JCAR 1986, 93).

Committee Members' Review

When and how do the committee members become involved in the review of proposed regulations? For most routine and noncontroversial regulations, the JCAR legislators' participation in rules review is largely confined to accepting or rejecting staff recommendations for objections to proposed rules that result from unresolved issues between the Committee's staff and the state agencies. Table 2 presents the four principal types of these staff recommendations for objection that the JCAR legislators have accepted since the Committee was first created in 1978. Collectively, these four types represent slightly more than 94 percent of the 965 objections to proposed general regulations issued by the Committee. Committee objections because of inadequate standards for the exercise of discretionary authority, the lack of regulatory clarity, and violations of general provisions of the IAPA account respectively, for

Table 2
Committee Objections by Type

Type	N	%
Statutory Authority and Legislative Intent	382	40
Standards for the Exercise of Discretionary Authority	226	23
Regulatory Clarity	168	17
IAPA-General Provisions	133	14

Note: For a discussion of the data used to create Table 2 see the Appendix.

23 percent, 17 percent, and 14 percent of all objections issued by the Committee.

The most interesting finding in Table 2 is the large volume of statutory authority objections. They represent the plurality of all objections ever issued by JCAR, and stand in sharp contrast to the small number of statutory authority questions asked during staff review. This sharp difference between the two levels of review suggests that while staff review may get bogged down in clarifying the language in proposed regulations, the actual staff recommendations taken to the JCAR legislators for their ratification more closely reflect the goals the General Assembly hoped to accomplish when it established the rules review process. This observation is reinforced by the nearly equal volume of committee objections that reflect the General Assembly's interest in regulatory relief. Regulatory clarity and discretionary standards objections, both of which are components of regulatory relief, account for 40 percent of all committee objections. Jointly, statutory authority, regulatory clarity, and discretionary standards objections account for 80 percent of all objections ever issued by JCAR and appear to reflect the General Assembly's two principal motives when it established the rules review process.

Nature and Original Intent

It is logical to assume that there should be a congruity between the nature of a rules review process and the reasons why a state legislature adopted it. As detailed in Chapter 3, the Illinois General Assembly originally sought a rules review process to prevent major statutory authority abuses in administrative rulemaking. By preventing such abuses from occurring, the Assembly hoped to reassert its constitutional lawmaking power and provide relief from overburdensome regulations to affected publics.

Tables 1 and 2 indicate that the nature of the rules review process in the Illinois General Assembly initially appears to implement these original purposes. Closer investigation, though, suggests that JCAR has implemented rules review in a manner at variance with the Assembly's original intent, that rules review does not focus primarily on identifying and remedying major statutory authority abuses. For example, as envisioned by the General Assembly, rules review does provide some degree of regulatory relief to the affected publics. But this relief is more procedural than substantive. The purposes that JCAR assigns to questions and objections concerning standards for discretionary authority underscore the procedural nature of the relief provided. These questions and objections are pursued to (1) make regulations less arbitrary; (2) provide increased certainty to the regulated publics as to the type and manner of administrative action that may be taken against them; and (3) provide the foundation for legal challenges to administrative action if an agency fails to follow the standards specified in its regulations (JCAR 1979, 244).

JCAR's approach to statutory authority further illustrates that the substance of rules review appears not to be in congruence with what the General Assembly originally intended. JCAR routinely focuses on prohibiting agencies from relying on implicit statutory authority as justification for provisions within their regulations rather than restricting its review to discovering major agency abuses of statutory authority as was intended by the General Assembly when it instituted rules review. JCAR justifies this variance by taking the position that a recognition of implicit statutory authority "weakens the ability of the legislature to control, or confine, the quasi-legislative rulemaking authority of agencies and [to] insure that agencies do not usurp legislative authority, or misinterpret legislative intent, which is a basic purpose of the legislative review process established under the Administrative Procedure Act" (JCAR 1980, 383).

Policy Neutral Review

The above discussion regarding JCAR staff questions and committee objections reveals that a rules review process may principally seek from state agencies accountability that is procedural and legal in its content. Such accountability appears to be policy neutral, not overtly challenging agencies on the substantive content or merit of their proposed regulations. JCAR legislators clearly emphasize this type of accountability in their definition of the Committee's role:

> JCAR is unique in that it is a legalistic committee. JCAR is not designed to make policy. Its purpose is to look for the intent of the legislature in proposed rules and to see if the agencies have the statutory authority to do the things they want to do. It is difficult for many legislators to keep this distinction between policy and legal authority separate. But even when JCAR approves of the policy within a proposed rule, the Committee must object if the agency violated legislative intent by not possessing the necessary statutory authority.

Policy neutral accountability is likely to be important to the continued existence of a rules review committee. Because its jurisdiction over state programs is likely to be so inclusive, a specially created rules review committee will probably encounter significant opposition from within the legislature. To produce some sort of tangible results without generating political opposition, a rules review committee needs an effective institutional perspective that "makes the committee *appear* to be approaching agency [regulations] from a special, limited frame of reference, thus avoiding the allegation that it is substituting its judgment for that of the authorization committees or the whole assembly" (Ethridge 1985, 144). One such perspective is a policy neutral rules review process that generally fails to question the substance or merit of proposed regulations. The Illinois experience with rules review underscores the utility of pursuing a policy neutral perspective.

As Chapter 3 makes clear, early in its own existence JCAR experienced opposition from a number of members of the General Assembly who feared that the Committee sought to substitute its will for that of the legislature as a whole. But there has been no serious legislative opposition to JCAR since 1980–81 when the

Committee succeeded in securing for itself the added authority to suspend an agency's proposed regulations. JCAR has minimized any opposition to itself by developing an institutional perspective that promotes the appearance of policy neutrality. This policy neutrality encourages an image that JCAR is sensitive to, and reflects the will of, the whole legislature.

This sensitivity manifests itself in the Committee's willingness to avoid adopting staff recommendations when its action could be perceived as preempting consideration by the full legislature or the appropriate authorizing committee. For example, at JCAR's December 1986 meeting, staff had prepared a recommendation for a committee objection to the Illinois Department of Mines and Minerals' proposed regulation to permit the detonation of explosive charges in underground mines while miners were working. The issue of "shooting on shifts" had generated controversy within the 1986 session of the General Assembly, but no political solution had been worked out. The debate was scheduled to continue in the 1987 spring session. So as not to preempt consideration by the full legislature, Representative Flinn suggested that JCAR take no action on the staff recommendation pertaining to this specific provision of the proposed regulation:

> The legislature made an attempt to deal with this in the Spring session, the House in particular . . . and after some time they decided to postpone the issue till Fall. . . . This issue is a very touchy one from the United Mine Workers, and the coal industry. The coal industry is in dire straits in the State of Illinois, and just about anything we do to harm them is going to harm the State as a whole. I would suggest that, if it is possible, the whole issue be dropped until next Spring when the legislature can address the issue of shooting on shifts (December 1986, 7).

Non-neutral Review

Despite the appearance of policy neutrality, the accountability pursued through rules review will not always be neutral. The

Illinois experience with rules review suggests three conditions under which presumably neutral review will actually not be neutral: (1) when a proposed regulation becomes salient to a legislator, on or off the reviewing committee, because of that regulation's potential impact on his or her constituency; (2) when interest groups representing the affected publics are allowed to intrude into the rules review process; or (3) when one of the purposes for rules review is regulatory relief.

As will be detailed more fully later in this chapter, rules review generally is not salient to most state legislators, either on or off the reviewing committee. But from time to time, when a proposed regulation appears likely to have a substantive impact upon a legislator's constituency or area of policy interest, the salience of rules review increases. Under these circumstances, a legislator is likely to express his or her concern about the proposed rule to the reviewing committee, or its staff, often with a request that a more thorough review than usual be conducted on that rule. Such a request is likely to result in staff recommendations being presented to the Committee so that the interested legislator can express his or her concern publicly and attempt to extract some consideration for this concern from the issuing agency.

An example of how increased saliency affects the neutrality of rules review is evident in the unsuccessful effort by one Illinois state senator to convince the Illinois Department of Agriculture to modify or withdraw its proposed regulation to change the traditional starting date of the Illinois State Fair. The new date conflicted with the schedules of 12 county fairs, one of which was in the senator's district, and he was concerned with the economic effect the proposed change would have on it. As part of his efforts to extract a compromise from the Department of Agriculture, the senator informed JCAR's executive director of his interest in the Department's proposed rule and the potential problem it would cause in his district. When the date change was finally reviewed by JCAR at its January 1987 meeting, the staff had prepared two recommendations for objection. The second objection closely paralleled the senator's concern regarding the economic impact of the date change on the affected county fairs. Though the recommendation was not accepted by the Committee, the fact that it was presented provided him the opportunity to publicly demonstrate to his constituents his opposition to the proposed change.

In an interview for this study, the senator candidly stated that his opposition to the Department of Agriculture's efforts to change the state fair's starting date had to do with its impact on the county fair in his district. His opposition had nothing to do with whether the Department had the legal authority to make the change. His opposition was not neutral but reflected a concern for the merit of the proposed date change and its impact on his district. Relatedly, JCAR staff review appears to have accommodated the senator's interest in the proposed regulation, suggesting that the neutrality of staff review is compromised when a regulation's salience to a committee member, or other legislator, is high.

Non-neutral rules review is also likely to occur whenever interest groups representing the affected publics are allowed to intrude into the process. Lobbying efforts designed to influence the final contents of proposed regulations and directed at the members and staff of the reviewing committee are the most common form of interest group intrusion. These lobbying efforts are not directed at the procedural content or legal authority of proposed regulations. Instead, they are directed toward a regulation's substantive policy content, and such concerns are clearly not neutral. For example, a spokesperson for the Illinois State Chamber of Commerce (ISCC) acknowledged that his organization gave early support for a rules review process. This support was partly because of the "extra club" it would provide the ISCC and other business organizations in their opposition to the social and environmental regulations that were being proposed by state agencies.

In Illinois, the concern over interest group intrusion into rules review was raised early on in JCAR's existence. For example, in 1979 during House debates on whether or not to grant JCAR a suspension power over proposed regulations, Rep. Arthur Greiman stressed that rules review had become a new access point for lobbyists: "I've been a member of that Committee and I've been lobbied. It's a new form of lobbying now. . . . And on . . . substantive issues, not just issues of procedure, not on the issues they [JCAR] should be considering, but on the substantive issues, on the wisdom of those issues" (House Bill 2351, June 27, 1980, 169).

JCAR legislators openly acknowledged that lobbying has become a regular feature of rules review. They maintained that most of the lobbying is less intense than elsewhere in the legislative process and largely restricted to providing information to the Committee as to where in the proposed regulation the interest group believes problems exist. One legislator equated lobbying JCAR to "strategic air strikes." He noted that with JCAR, unlike the lobbying in the general legislative process, interest groups have a limited range of operations because the Committee cannot formally amend regulations. This reduces the role of interest groups to informing the committee members and the staff as to what they believe is wrong with the proposed regulation. Through this information, JCAR may find a basis on which to object, and the objection may result in the issuing agency modifying or withdrawing the proposed regulation. Even this limited lobbying is likely to influence the substantive content of a proposed regulation or delay its implementation, as the National Association of Black Social Workers' (Chicago Chapter) ability to delay the transracial adoption regulations of the Illinois Department of Children and Family Services clearly illustrates.

In 1985, the Department had in force a transracial adoption regulation requiring that before a child of one race could be placed with adopting parents of another race a six-month search had to be conducted for suitable adoptive parents of the child's race. This provision of the regulation was challenged in a complaint filed with the United States Department of Health and Human Services Office of Civil Rights. In the complaint filed by prospective adopting Caucasian parents of a non–Caucasian child, it was alleged that the Department's transracial adoption regulation violated Title VII of the 1964 Civil Rights Act and was therefore discriminatory. In a compliance agreement with the Department of Health and Human Services, the Department of Children and

Family Services agreed to eliminate any placement policies that discriminated against the race of prospective adopting parents.

To fulfill its legal obligation under the compliance agreement, the Department amended its transracial adoption rule through the normal procedures of the IAPA and solicited public comments. It was not until after the public comment period had expired, and JCAR's staff had completed its review and found nothing objectionable about the amendment, that the National Association of Black Social Workers wrote to JCAR's executive director to voice its opposition to the proposed amendment. In a letter to the executive director, which was also sent to all committee members, the Association sought to prevent the implementation of the amendment removing the race of the prospective parent as a factor in determining the placement of children available for adoption. The Association alleged that the proposed amendment would have a "negative impact on the future of Black and other minority children in the State of Illinois," and it requested that JCAR postpone approving the amended regulation until it had the opportunity to confer with the Committee and the Department (Webb 1986).

At its August 1986 meeting, the Committee concurred with the Association's request and postponed final committee decision on the regulation for 30 days so that "the staff and DCFS [could] work out their differences" (JCAR August 1986, 21). But there were no differences to work out with JCAR's staff. The staff had recommended to the Committee that the Department be given a Certificate of No Objection. The differences that had to be worked out were the policy disagreements between the National Association of Black Social Workers and the Department of Children and Family Services. In effect, the Association had successfully used the rules review process to gain additional access to the Department of Children and Family Services and to delay the final implementation of the transracial adoption regulation.

Finally, rules review undertaken for the purpose of providing regulatory relief is, in and of itself, non-neutral. Such review is biased in favor of the regulated public. In Illinois, this bias gives particular advantage to the business community as JCAR seeks to protect it from overburdensome regulations. This bias has the potential of undermining legitimate administrative interest and lessening the protection for those publics that the regulations were originally designed to protect. The Illinois Department of Commerce and Community Affairs' regulation discussed earlier that pertained to a grant program for local tourism and convention boards illustrates the impact of this bias. Had the Department modified or withdrawn this regulation prior to obtaining specific legislative authorization for the objectionable provisions, the regulatory burden on the local bureaus would have, indeed, been decreased. But, the Department's interest in preventing the misuse of program funds and not underwriting the entire promotional budgets of these local bureaus would have been jeopardized.

Relatedly, had the Illinois Department of Children and Family Services responded favorably in its Relative Home Placement regulations to JCAR's 42 questions pertaining to agency personnel use of discretionary authority, the regulatory burden on relative foster parents would likewise have been lessened. The Department's acquiescence would have meant that these foster parents would have had a clear statement of the obligation they were assuming. But, the children for whom the regulations were designed to protect and for whom the Department was responsible would have received less protection. The more specifically stated criteria for the exercise of discretionary authority would have meant that department personnel would have had less freedom in responding to the needs of the children assigned to relative foster homes.

EXPLAINING THE ACCOUNTABILITY SOUGHT

The relevance to other aspects of legislative life that rules review has for the JCAR legislators, and the dominant role of the committee staff to the process, appears to account for the nature of rules review in Illinois or, more precisely, for the accountability sought from state agencies through the process. Both of these characteristics are basic to understanding rules review in Illinois, and are also likely to be among the dominant factors in any rules review process, though admittedly in different configurations.

Two types of legislators are likely to be found on a rules review committee, those for whom the process is relevant to other aspects of their legislative life and those for whom it is not. Legislators of the first type may be described as oversight legislators, already predisposed toward overseeing and controlling administrative behavior (Rosenthal 1981b). In particular, these oversight legislators (1) "want to know more about policies, programs, and agencies . . . in order to develop their own knowledge and expertise"; (2) "want to improve the performance of state government"; and (3) are institutional men and women "who have a commitment to the legislature and the legislative process" (Rosenthal 1981a, 126–127).

A small number of these oversight legislators are found on JCAR. These legislators remain on the Committee well after their initial two-year appointment. For example, Sen. Prescott Bloom had been a continuous member of JCAR from its inception in 1978 until his untimely death in 1986. Similarly, Rep. Monroe Flinn has also been a nearly continuous member, having served on JCAR continuously except for the two years he spent in the Illinois House Democratic leadership. Legislators like Bloom and Flinn take an active role in the Committee's work, are largely responsible for JCAR's effectivenes when a major abuse in an agency's rulemaking is uncovered and needs correction, and appear genuinely concerned about the institutional well-being of the General Assembly.

For these oversight legislators, JCAR provides the opportunity to focus on lawmaking over representation. As one JCAR legislator observed: "JCAR makes me a better lawmaker. It provides me an opportunity to serve the people of Illinois and not just my district. Here, I'm a 100 percent lawmaker. Outside of JCAR, I'm more of a representative for my district." Participating in rules review also seems to provide these legislators with a better understanding of what their job actually entails. One of these legislators observed that as a freshman he believed that his job began and ended with the passage of legislation. But after being on the Committee, he now understands that he must be concerned with the implementation of legislation as well as its passage. Finally, because of its broad jurisdiction, JCAR educates these oversight legislators on a wide array of policies and programs with which they might not otherwise have become familiar. As one legislator observed, his tenure on JCAR has allowed him to "get into the nitty-gritty of the government process."

Legislators for whom the process is not relevant are also likely to be found on a rules review committee. Unlike oversight legislators, this group of legislators is more likely to be motivated by typical legislative orientations such as reelection, constituency service, or increased influence within the legislature (Fenno 1973, Chapter 2; Ripley 1983, Chapter 1; Smith and Deering 1984, Chapter 4). Because so few oversight legislators exist, it is even possible that this type of legislator will dominate the rules review process. The rules review process in Illinois is one such example.

The oversight legislators on JCAR rarely number more than three to five of the 12 committee members. For most of the JCAR legislators, the Committee lacks relevance because it appears to be only peripherally related to most other aspects of their legislative lives. For example, a portion of the JCAR legislators believed that special expertise is needed to participate in rules review and that the Committee should be the special province of legislators who are also lawyers. As one JCAR legislator put it: "It's simply easier to participate in a committee that is considering raising an agency's appropriation by 5 percent than it is to participate in a JCAR meeting." Another JCAR legislator observed: "Rules review should be made more relevant to a legislator's other responsibilities. It always bothered me that at our meetings we only heard from committee staff and the agencies. I would have liked to open the process up for participation from lobbyists and other affected parties. I wanted to make JCAR more like regular committee meetings." Perhaps a former JCAR deputy director stated most succinctly why rules review lacks relevance for many JCAR legislators: "A legislator doesn't win reelection in Moline by being on JCAR."

The lack of relevance that rules review may have for many of the legislators on a reviewing committee can impact upon the process in several important ways. First, turnover on such a committee is likely to be high. For example, in Illinois, the average committee tenure between 1978 and 1986 for JCAR legislators was only three years, and it is not uncommon for JCAR legislators to ask not to be reappointed, or at least, not to actively seek reassignment to the Committee. As one former JCAR legislator observed: "I asked not to be reappointed. JCAR just didn't fit my personality. The Committee was just too legal and statistical, and I'd rather be a mover and a shaker, creating policy rather than confronting the details of implementation."

Second, it is probable that attendance at committee meetings will be low, and for those who do attend, their actual participation in the committee's business is likely to be of a poor quality. For example, JCAR legislators acknowledge that attendance at the monthly meetings is often poor. In fact, two JCAR legislators who served on the Committee during the course of this study had never attended a single meeting during their two-year appointment. Other JCAR legislators who did attend the Committee's monthly meetings admit to being more like observers than participants. As one former JCAR legislator put it: "At the monthly meetings, I was a very good listener." Another JCAR legislator observed:

> My participation at monthly meetings is poor. I'm more often involved in trying to stay awake. Often I'm not prepared for the meetings. I should be but I'm not. I get the material soon enough but I only skim through it. The material is so boring and tedious to read. It's like reading a sociology text. It's not that you don't understand it, but that it's so dry. You start to read it, and your mind wanders here and there.

Third, because of rules review's general lack of relevance, it is possible that legislators who serve on a reviewing committee will be heavily dependent upon the committee's staff for support and direction. Such dependency is clearly evident among the JCAR legislators. As one of these legislators observed:

> Staff controls whether we object to a proposed regulation or not. When I was on the Committee, there was very little independent thinking taking place on the part of the members. Staff generally told us when we needed to object, and we did so. Staff control at JCAR is stronger than on any other committee. Part of this is due to the Committee's subject matter. At JCAR meetings, we'd go through a whole thick volume of fairly tedious materials and after you'd sat through a few of these meetings, it became easy to let staff do it for you.

JCAR legislators' observations regarding their dependence on staff are supported by the high rate at which the committee members accept staff recommendations for objections to proposed regulations. In 1984, the Committee accepted nearly 69 percent of all staff recommendations for objections. In 1985, this percentage rose to 77 percent, and in 1986, it increased again to 80 percent. Overall, for these three years, the JCAR legislators accepted 76 percent of all staff recommendations for objections.

Committee Staff Dominance

Previous research has established that staff is likely to be influential in any legislative process where the subject matter is (1) specific and technical; (2) perceived by legislators as being unrelated to other legislative concerns; and (3) characterized by legislative indifference to the process (Rosenthal 1981b, 229). The discussion concluding the previous section appears to confirm that these findings can also be generalized to rules review. But these comments further suggest that staff may be more than influential in the process. They suggest that excessive committee dependence on staff for direction and guidance may lead to actual staff dominance of rules review.

Rules review in Illinois clearly appears to be such a staff-
dominated process. But this staff dominance is of a particular kind.
It is dominance by JCAR's executive director, Bruce Johnson, and
his staff management team, rather than dominance by committee
staff as a whole. This centrality of the upper echelon of JCAR's
staff is clearly evident in the observations of JCAR legislators cited
above, the lower echelon staff, and agency officials responsible for
rules review within their departments. For example, one JCAR
legislator observed: "Part of the control staff exerts is due to the
executive director. He's a very confident guy who is viewed as one
of the founding fathers of rules review in Illinois."

Former staff persons also noted that during their tenure the rules
analysts and staff attorneys were allowed almost no interaction
with the committee members. Because of their isolation from the
committee members, many of these former rules analysts and staff
attorneys believe that they did not represent the legislators' outlook
toward rules review. Instead, former staff asserts that the orientation permeating the rules review process is that of the executive
director. The importance of Director Johnson's orientation toward
rules review was summed up by one former staff person with the
observation: "He is the staff."

Agency representatives who regularly interact with JCAR also
perceive the executive director and his staff management team
as the persons most central to rules review. Agency representatives perceive the centrality of the executive director and
his staff management team because their experiences with
JCAR's staff suggest that the rules analysts and staff attorneys
are closely supervised by staff management and have very little
independent authority in how they conduct their review. One
agency representative who had interacted with JCAR for several
years observed:

> I find that the staff is much more open-minded than the
> management. But the reviewer cannot commit to whether
> any changes to our regulations proposed in our meetings
> will actually be acceptable to his supervisors. What's frus-

trating in all of this is that the department does not deal with the people at JCAR who are responsible for the actual decisions.

As further evidence of Director Johnson and his staff management team's centrality to rules review, the agency representatives also noted how the monthly meetings changed over time from deliberative exchanges between the JCAR legislators and themselves to the nearly automatic and uncritical acceptance of staff recommendations:

> In the beginning there was a lot more dialogue between the agencies and the committee members. Staff recommendations weren't so automatically accepted, and the agencies were actually listened to. But now we needn't even bother to show up at the monthly meetings because the committee members accept almost all of the staff recommendations presented to them without questions.

The ability or potential for committee staff to dominate a rules review process should not be understated, because whoever controls what rules review is controls the accountability that the process seeks from state agencies. It is possible that through this control committee staff may manipulate the substance of rules review to promote its own organizational purposes rather than those originally put forth by the state legislature. For example, there is at least circumstantial evidence suggesting that JCAR's executive director and his staff management team manipulate rules review for their own organization's goals rather than those established by the General Assembly. In particular, they appear to manipulate rules review to insure their continued organizational survival.

First, Director Johnson and his staff management team appear to seek a clientele other than the General Assembly. In particular, there is a concerted effort to service the Illinois business community and gain support for JCAR within it. For example, since 1983 JCAR's staff has published a weekly newsletter designed to alert small businesses of proposed regulations that may affect them. This newsletter, which is not authorized by the IAPA, is sent free of cost to any individual, business, or association that requests to be placed on the mailing list. The information contained in the newsletter is largely repetitive of that found in the *Illinois Register*. The main distinction is that the *Illinois Register* has an annual subscription price of $200. JCAR staff defends this cultivation of small businesses and other subscribers to the newsletter as part of the "Committee's commitment to alerting the general public to their responsibilities and privileges available pursuant to the Illinois Administrative Procedure Act" (JCAR 1984, 10).

Second, Director Johnson and his staff management team promote their own organizational survival by neutralizing administrative opposition to rules review. This is accomplished by insuring that the substance of rules review is noncontroversial and policy neutral, except when proposed regulations are salient to one or more JCAR legislators or other members of the General Assembly. As the previous discussion clearly indicates, the substance of rules review is generally noncontroversial, focusing not on the substantive merit of a proposed regulation but upon content clarification and copyediting. A former member of JCAR's management staff reports that a conscious decision was made earlier in JCAR's existence not to question the agencies on the substantive content of their proposed rules and to focus on the noncontroversial. This decision was made to reduce potential administrative opposition to JCAR and to avoid unwanted conflicts. This decision was made despite provisions in the IAPA that appear to authorize JCAR to conduct a substantive policy-oriented review of proposed regulations.

A review that focuses on content clarification rather than substance makes rules review a safe process in that state agencies are held accountable only for the form that their regulations take. In most instances where the proposed rule has no legislative saliency, JCAR is "just another hoop" for the state agencies to jump through in order to get their regulations adopted. The minor impact rules review normally has on their regulations does not seem to warrant a concerted administrative branch effort to reduce JCAR's "procedural harassment" of the agencies. As one agency representative observed: "Rules review is an irritation and nuisance for most state agencies. The process results in few substantive changes in our rules, and for this reason alone, JCAR isn't worth the expenditure of political capital that would be necessary to change the process."

Third, JCAR's executive director and staff management team additionally promote their own organizational survival by nurturing an impression among the JCAR legislators that the state agencies still routinely abuse their rulemaking authority. This appears to be accomplished by continuing to present large numbers of staff recommendations for objections to the committee members. Since committee members uncritically accept staff recommendations, a correspondingly high volume of objections persists. As Table 3 demonstrates, the number of objections issued by JCAR throughout the years has not declined. To the contrary, after a plateau, there was a sharp upward movement beginning in 1982. In 1978, the first year JCAR was in full operation, 72 objections were issued to 507 regulations. If one objection per rule is assumed, it is as if JCAR objected to 14 percent of all regulations proposed by the state agencies. In contrast, 298 objections were issued in 1986 to 818 regulations. Again, assuming one objection per rule, this is as if the Committee objected to 36 percent of all proposed regulations.

Table 3
Number of Objections Issued by JCAR

Year	'78	'79	'80	'81	'82	'83	'84	'85	'86
Number of Objections	72	65	55	62	98	156	300	159	298
Number of Rules	507	586	682	731	615	650	704	634	818

Note: For a discussion of the data used to create Table 3 see the Appendix.

Maintaining such a high volume of objections is contrary to the conventional wisdom regarding the effect that rules review has on agency rulemaking. The number of objections issued by a rules review committee should be high initially when a rules review process is new. But the volume of objections should decline as the state agencies become more accustomed to having their regulations reviewed by the legislature. The continued presence of rules review begins to serve as a moderating influence on the agencies, reducing their misinterpretations of legislative intent, statutory authority, and other provisions of a state's administrative procedure act (Jones 1982, 8). But as Table 3 shows, this moderating influence does not appear to have taken place in Illinois. Instead, the number of objections issued by JCAR gives the impression that the state agencies still routinely abuse their rulemaking authority despite nearly ten years of an ongoing rules review process. By encouraging this impression, a belief persists within the General Assembly—or at least among the JCAR legislators—that rules review is a legislative task worth retaining.

Agency Responsiveness to Rules Review

INTRODUCTION

The nature of rules review reveals the substance of the accountability that a state legislature seeks from administrative agencies in regard to their rulemaking. But there is no guarantee that the accountability sought will be actually achieved. Most rules review committees exercise only advisory authority over proposed regulations. Therefore, to secure the accountability it seeks from the state agencies, a typical rules review committee is principally dependent upon those agencies' voluntary responsiveness to the process. Like oversight generally, the effectiveness of rules review is "dependent . . . on the acquiescence of the bureaucrats involved" (Gruber 1987, 86). The Illinois experience suggests why an agency may or may not choose to be responsive to rules review. It also suggests that despite the need for agency acquiescence to rules review, how a state legislature constructs and implements the process can greatly encourage or discourage agency responsiveness to it.

COMMITTEE OBJECTIONS

A principal indicator of agency responsiveness to rules review in Illinois is the agencies' voluntary compliance with committee objections. This compliance is demonstrated by the agencies modifying or withdrawing their proposed regulations in light of JCAR's objections. For the first eight years of JCAR's existence, state agencies have complied with only 53 percent of all committee objections.

The state agencies' compliance with committee objections is also characterized by a good deal of divergence across the eight years. In 1978, JCAR's first year of existence, agencies modified or withdrew their regulations in response to 67 percent of committee objections. In 1979 and 1980, compliance declined and hovered around the 50 percent mark. In 1981, compliance improved dramatically, rising to 67 percent. It continued to rise in 1982, peaking at 73 percent. But since 1983, agency compliance with committee objections has declined steadily, and, in 1985, it reached a low point of only 38 percent. As one JCAR legislator observed, this low compliance rate suggests that "committee objections may do very little to change the agencies' attitudes toward rulemaking."

Agency voluntary compliance also varies depending upon the type of objection that is issued to the agencies. To demonstrate this variance, agency compliance with committee objections to proposed general rulemakings has been calculated for 14 Illinois executive departments and independent agencies for the combined years 1978–85. Table 4 reports these compliance rates for three of the four principal types of objections that were discussed in Chapter 4: (1) statutory authority; (2) standards for the exercise of discretionary authority; and (3) regulatory clarity.

Table 4
Voluntary Compliance by Type of Objection

Type	Number of Objections	Number of Withdraws / Modifies	Percent Compliance
Statutory Authority	152	43	28
Standards	110	68	62
Regulatory	52	29	56

Note: For a discussion of the data used to create Table 4 see the Appendix .

The most striking observation drawn from Table 4 is the remarkably low level at which state agencies comply with committee objections that question the statutory authority of their proposed regulations. Agencies agree to withdraw or modify rules objected to on these grounds only 28 percent of the time. Considering that a principal reason for establishing rules review is to insure that state agencies abide by statutory authority, this low level of compliance is a significant finding. It suggests that advisory rules review may be unable to project the reviewing committee's interpretation of statutory authority onto the state agencies. If this is indeed the case, advisory rules review may not be an effective means by which a state legislature can reclaim and maintain its preeminence over state lawmaking.

In contrast to agency nonresponsiveness to statutory authority objections, Table 4 shows that Illinois state agencies are reasonably responsive to objections seeking procedural regulatory clarity. The state agencies agree to withdraw or modify proposed regulations in 62 percent of all standards objections and 56 percent of all regulatory clarity objections. As will be discussed later, this divergence between compliance with statutory authority objections and other types of objections is due, in part, to the higher "cost" associated with agency compliance with statutory authority objections.

To this point, the discussion seems to indicate a general lack of agency responsiveness to rules review as evidenced by low level of formal compliance with committee objections. An important caveat, though, needs to be discussed. Legislators who serve on a rules review committee that issues objections to proposed regulations may not interpret these objections as placing authoritative demands upon the agencies. In this situation, the members of the reviewing committee are likely to place less significance on formal compliance with committee objections than on whether or not the issue that caused the objection is somehow corrected. Such is the case with the JCAR legislators.

Most JCAR legislators do not see objections as placing authoritative demands upon the agencies. As one committee member put it: "We're not out to bash any heads with our objections." Instead,

JCAR legislators generally share the sentiments expressed by one of the more senior members of the Committee:

> An objection is not a reprimand, or a refusal to let an agency promulgate its rules. It's more like a legislative scolding and warning that the agency runs the risk of being publicly embarrassed by corrective legislation, or some other means, if it implements its rule as proposed. Objections are our way of getting the agency's attention.

The JCAR legislators' mild outlook toward committee objections is matched by an equally mild outlook toward formal agency compliance with these objections. The consensus of most of these legislators is that formal compliance is not necessary as long as the situation that prompted the objections is somehow alleviated. Formal agency compliance is seen as only one of several acceptable ways that proposed regulations are made accountable to the legislature. For example, instead of withdrawing or modifying their rules, state agencies may agree to seek additional authorizing legislation when the committee objections pertain to statutory authority.

A second option is for the reviewing committee to introduce its own corrective legislation when the agencies fail to rectify the conditions that prompted the original objection to their proposed rules. This is the course most often pursued by JCAR. Between 1978 and 1986, JCAR drafted 200 pieces of legislation for consideration by the Illinois General Assembly. Of these 200 bills, 164 have directly concerned inadequacies discovered through JCAR's review of proposed regulations, and they have generally sought to correct problems not resolved through formal agency compliance with committee objections. This use of corrective legislation is explored more fully in Chapter 6.

EXPLAINING AGENCY RESPONSIVENESS

The above discussion suggests that Illinois state agencies appear only marginally responsive to JCAR and rules review, and therefore only marginally responsive to the Illinois General Assembly.

Obviously, the agency responsiveness in Illinois may not be generalized to other rules review processes. But the factors that explain agency responsiveness in Illinois can be stated as analytic generalizations that may then help to understand agency responsiveness in other state rules review processes. The five factors that explain the nature of agency responsiveness to the Illinois rules review process are (1) the lack of relevance that rules review has for many JCAR legislators; (2) the general absence of effective sanctions that can be applied to unresponsive agencies; (3) the working relationship between JCAR and state agencies; (4) a review process that is at variance with the original intentions of the General Assembly; and (5) agency costs associated with responsiveness.

Lack of Relevance

Agency responsiveness to rules review is likely to be directly related to the level of relevance that the process holds for those legislators appointed to the reviewing committee. The JCAR legislators' behavior toward rules review discussed in Chapter 4 suggests that legislators elsewhere may not perceive any relevance between their participation in rules review and other aspects of their legislative life. This lack of relevance is likely to impact negatively on committee tenure, expertise, and level of committee members' participation in rules review. Additionally, it may allow rules review to become a staff driven and dominated process.

As is the case in Illinois, state agencies will likely be aware of this lack of relevance and the resulting dominance of committee staff. Jointly, these two conditions define for the agencies to whom they are actually being made accountable. This perception helps to determine their responsiveness to rules review. As one agency representative observed:

> Rarely does this department withdraw or modify a rule in response to JCAR's objections. The Committee's own behavior has generally diminished the significance of an agency receiving an objection. The committee members so

readily accept staff recommendations without any questions that the overall importance of an objection is greatly
reduced, and the agencies come to realize that it is JCAR's
staff that we actually have to satisfy.

Availability of Sanctions

Agency responsiveness is likely to be directly related to the
availability of formal and informal sanctions that can be applied,
or threatened to be applied, against nonresponsive state agencies.
Rules review in most state legislatures is advisory. The committees
responsible for review are generally without any formal sanctions
that can be applied against nonresponsive agencies. Even when a
rules review committee does possess formal sanctions, such as the
legislative veto, the actual availability and utility of that sanction
may be questionable.

For example, in 1981 JCAR acquired the power to suspend
agency regulations for 180 days pending approval by the full
General Assembly. Initially, the potential threat of a legislative veto
seemed to encourage greater agency responsiveness. As previously
observed, agency compliance with committee objections jumped
dramatically in 1981 and 1982 after JCAR obtained the power to
suspend proposed regulations. In a 1982 interview, Sen. Prescott
Bloom underscored the initial importance and impact of this
legislative veto:

> When the Joint Committee first came into existence, the
> agencies responded to our objections about two-thirds of
> the time. After they found out that we had no teeth, their
> response rate went way down. We felt that we needed a
> hammer over the agencies and the budget process is just
> too cumbersome. Although the veto has been used only
> twice in 18 months, the agencies are more willing to listen.
> (Jones 1982, 9)

But this suspension power has proven to be a largely impotent
sanction. Despite the initial impact of the legislative veto noted
previously, its enhancement of agency responsiveness has dimin-

ished because not enough JCAR legislators regularly attend the Committee's monthly meetings to allow the legislative veto to be exercised. The relationship between poor meeting attendance and the utility of the legislative veto has not been lost on either the state agencies or the JCAR legislators. One agency representative noted that the suspension authority is of minor consequence to his agency because "it's clear that JCAR cannot get the three-fifths attendance at its meeting that is necessary before the Committee can suspend an agency's rule." In a similar vein, a former JCAR legislator observed: "When I was on the Committee, our limited power to force compliance was one of my concerns. I would have liked to have prohibited a number of rules from being filed, but we couldn't. With such low attendance among some of the members, we just didn't have the votes necessary to suspend them."

The utility of JCAR's suspension power to bolster agency compliance is further diminished by its dubious constitutionality resulting from the United States Supreme Court ruling in *Immigration and Naturalization Service v. Chadha*. Because of this, JCAR is hesitant to use its suspension power. The observation of one JCAR legislator underscores how the loss of the legislative veto has affected the agencies' willingness to comply with committee objections: "Ever since the Supreme Court decided against the congressional use of the legislative veto, there has been a reluctance at JCAR to use it. The combination of *Chadha* and our own reluctance to exercise the suspension authority has resulted in a corresponding decline in agency compliance with our objections."

Though a rules review committee may not possess formal sanctions, its members can use informal sanctions to encourage agencies' responsiveness. Committee members can clearly threaten to apply sanctions available to them elsewhere in the legislature to nonresponsive agencies. The sanction that agencies are most likely to fear is one that threatens their appropriations.

The Illinois agency representatives report fearing any threats made by JCAR legislators to their agencies' appropriations for failure to comply with committee objections. Agency representatives acknowledge that the responsiveness of their agency to

JCAR's review is determined in part by the significance that individual JCAR legislators attach to agency responsiveness with specific objections, and the potential for retaliation if this responsiveness is not forthcoming.

> The significance of an objection, and the decision whether to comply with it or not, depends upon its content and political motivation. The more politically motivated it appears to be, the greater the likelihood that this agency will comply with it. We don't want to antagonize legislators who may retaliate against us elsewhere in the legislative process. For this reason, it's important to get a sense of just how important an objection is to the committee members, and what significance they attach to our actual compliance. They may object to your rules, but, if you pay attention, they will also show you whether they really care if you comply or not.

A second agency representative observed:

> More often than not, we don't place a great deal of significance on an objection from JCAR. Most of the time an objection only means that we have to write a response to it. It's a pretty rare occurrence that we feel that it is necessary to modify or withdraw a rule because JCAR has objected to it. Instances do arise, though, where for purely political reasons, such as if it's appropriation time, where we don't want to run the risk of antagonizing any legislator. In these instances, we more carefully consider our decisions as to how to respond to JCAR.

Relationship Between the Agencies and the Reviewing Committee

The nature of the working relationship between the state agencies and the reviewing committee may also impact upon agency responsiveness to rules review. In particular, the more cooperative and less adversarial this relationship is, the more responsive state agencies are likely to be. In Illinois, the working relationship between JCAR and the state agencies is adversarial, resulting in decreased agency responsiveness.

Agency representatives observe that staff review is characterized by an anti-agency mentality that presumes that the agencies consciously and intentionally abuse their rulemaking authority:

> [S]taff review is colored by a suspicion that the agencies are trying to pull something over on the legislature. You can see it in the questions the staff ask, and all it does is to create an adversary situation where none needs to exist. In response to it all, the agencies just grow more indifferent to the whole process.

Agency representatives attribute the adversariness in rules review to JCAR's executive director. Former JCAR staff also noted the overly adversarial nature of the relationship between state agencies and the Committee and, like the agency representatives, they too attributed responsibility for this condition to JCAR's executive director and his staff management team. In particular, former staff persons observed that the committee's staff management fostered an antibureaucracy mentality by encouraging them to approach rules review as if state agencies were likely to abuse their rulemaking authority, both in writing regulations and in implementing them. Typical of their comments is the following observation:

> I regard the major problem of the Joint Committee's review to be the excessive intransigence in its negotiations with the agencies. The negotiating atmosphere can be unnecessarily adversarial. There is a mentality at the supervisory level that when a question is asked a change should almost inevitably follow. This translates into an unwillingness to accept adequate agency justificatons for a provision of its rules, or to effect trivial changes in the rules.

It is reasonable for JCAR to pursue an adversarial relationship with state agencies that are routinely unresponsive to its review. But as the agency representatives observed, the Committee, particularly in staff review, does not discriminate in its suspicions between those agencies that have an alleged history of being nonresponsive and of abusing their rulemaking authority and those agencies that do not: "Our agency has probably worked harder and closer with JCAR than any other agency. . . . But our willingness to make changes and to accept the legitimacy of JCAR's role isn't met with a corresponding reduction in staff's suspicion of us. We're still treated as if we are out to abuse our rulemaking authority." The practical outcome of JCAR's nondiscriminating adversariness appears to be a decreased willingness on the part of some agencies to be responsive to staff review: "Because we've seen no fruit from our willingness to cooperate, we've recently reassessed our relationship with JCAR, and we're beginning to cooperate less. . . . In retaliation, staff appears to be recommending an increasing number of objections against our rules."

Responsiveness and Original Intent

State agencies are more likely to be responsive to a rules review process that they perceive is being implemented as the state legislature intended, rather than a process that is not so implemented. In Illinois, the agency representatives accept the right of the General Assembly to oversee their rulemaking authority. Indeed, they generally agree that rules review can be potentially beneficial in insuring the responsible exercise of that authority. They agree with the observation that "rules review can assure that as unelected bureaucrats we are held accountable for our rulemaking; and in regard to statutory authority, someone should be watching over us."

Despite abstract acceptance, most agency representatives believe that JCAR's implementation of rules review is at odds with the original intentions of the General Assembly. They maintain that in creating rules review, the General Assembly intended it to be a process by which the legislature could oversee administrative rulemaking to prevent major abuses in the agencies' statutory authority and to insure that regulations reflected legislative intent. Contrary to this original intention, the agency representatives perceive that JCAR has implemented a review process that is preoccupied with the "form" of proposed regulations. By form, the agency representatives are referring to procedural regulatory relief, or what the agencies have dubbed "procedural harassment."

The agencies' perception of JCAR's implementation of rules review is at least circumstantially substantiated in Chapter 4 and the discussion regarding the nature of rules review and original intent. A 1983 internal JCAR staff task report also verifies the agencies' perception:

> [T]he overwhelming opinion among the Joint Committee's own professional staff is that . . . the Joint Committee is exceeding the bounds of oversight intended in the statutory directive that the Committee insure that rules are in "proper form" by asking too many questions directed simply at rewording rules or making minor changes which do not improve the rules in a meaningful way. (JCAR 1983, 15)

The practical outcome of the agencies' perception of JCAR's implementation of rules review is to undermine the potential effectiveness of the process as a means of promoting bureaucratic responsiveness. In particular, "staff time is diverted from more important problems of legislative oversight" and "the Joint Committee's image and relationship with the agencies deteriorates as reviewers become, in the view of the agencies, pedantic copy editors rather than guardians of the legislative will" (JCAR 1983, 15–16).

Agency "Costs" Associated with Responsiveness

Agency responsiveness to rules review is likely to be directly affected by the costs to an agency's program if it revises a proposed regulation in light of review. What these costs might be is clearly articulated in the observation of the agency representatives interviewed for this study:

> Objections based upon such things as inadequate standards are fairly easy to comply with. In these instances, we really aren't giving up very much, and they can be complied with by revising the language to accommodate JCAR's objections. But when JCAR objects to our rules because they lack statutory authority, it's much more difficult to comply. . . . Here, our choices are fairly limited. Unlike other types of objections, we can't simply redraft the wording of the rule. If we comply, it means that we must give up provisions in the rules that we feel are important to the successful implementation of the program. If we don't formally comply, but agree to seek corrective legislation to explicitly grant us the disputed authority we already believe we possess, we expend resources that would be better spent elsewhere. In addition, if we enforce the disputed provision while we seek the appropriate corrective legislation, it appears that the agency is enforcing rules it has admitted it does not have the authority to promulgate. In either case, we are often better off in not complying with the objection.

In short, staff questions and committee objections pertaining to procedural regulatory relief impose few costs on the agencies because they require agencies only to rework the language of the proposed regulations. In contrast, statutory authority objections and questions are extremely difficult for agencies to comply with because responsiveness to these objections and questions is too costly. They require agencies to give up provisions of the regulations deemed necessary to the successful implementation of the affected programs.

A Credible Process

Each of the five factors discussed above is likely to contribute to whether or not agencies are responsive to rules review. Agencies may accept the right of a state legislature to review their proposed regulations. But these five factors underscore that for responsiveness to be forthcoming the agencies must perceive the review process as being credible. To achieve this credibility and secure agency responsiveness, a state legislature must pay close attention to how the process is implemented. In particular, a state legislature needs to implement rules review so that it (1) is perceived to be salient and relevant to legislators; (2) possesses sanctions that can be imposed on agencies that are not voluntarily responsive; (3) minimizes agency costs associated with responsiveness; (4) emphasizes cooperation between the oversight committee and the agencies; and (5) (if implemented by an institutional oversight committee) does not pursue goals at variance with those set by the whole legislature.

6

Agency Responsiveness, Rules Review, and Corrective Legislation

INTRODUCTION

In a rules review process, agency responsiveness to the reviewing committee's objections to proposed regulations is only one way in which accountability for administrative rulemaking is sought. As Chapter 5 suggests, a rules review committee may choose to secure administrative accountability by introducing into the state legislature legislation designed to correct those rulemaking deficiencies discovered during its review of a department's proposed regulations. An analysis of JCAR's legislative activities for the years 1978–86 suggests at least three types of corrective legislation available to a rules review committee in its pursuit of accountable rulemaking.

First, a reviewing committee may introduce legislation to expand or clarify an agency's statutory authority in order to retrospectively authorize regulations that the agency has already implemented. Such corrective legislation is likely to take place when the reviewing committee is in substantive agreement with the rulemaking activities of an agency, but feels its statutory authority for the regulations is vague and unclear. Second, the corrective legislation may direct an agency to issue specific regulations that publicly state agency policy in a particular area and develop standards by which the agency's discretionary authority will be exercised.

Third, a reviewing committee may choose to introduce corrective legislation that revokes regulations adopted and implemented over committee objections. Revocation legislation extracts the most severe form of accountability from state agencies and represents the most serious threat to an agency's regulations and rulemaking activities. The serious implications of revocation legislation is illustrated by the unlikelihood of its frequent use. For example, from 1978 to 1986, JCAR legislators introduced only five pieces of revocation legislation into the General Assembly. Four of these have occurred since 1983 and the Supreme Court decision in *Immigration and Naturalization Service v. Chadha* striking down the legislative veto. The more frequent reliance upon revocation legislation after *Chadha* suggests that, at least in Illinois, it may be evolving into a legislative alternative to the legislative veto.

In an advisory review process, the use of corrective legislation underscores that rules review is likely to be most effective when the process is used as a means of information-gathering for the whole legislature rather than as the process that directly holds the state agencies accountable for their rulemaking. In this capacity, a rules review committee identifies areas where rulemaking authority needs revision and makes recommendations to the full legislature for its consideration.

Corrective legislation also promotes a rules review committee's own internal accountability to its parent body. As Chapter 3 demonstrates, the power and authority of the reviewing committee vis-à-vis the legislature can be a genuine concern to the latter. But corrective legislation provides the whole legislature an opportunity to review and approve the actions of the rules review committee. In the course of this review, the likelihood that the rules review committee will be able to substitute its will for that of the full legislature is reduced.

A rules review process that relies upon corrective legislation to secure accountable rulemaking is also promoting the juridical principle or, more simply put, the rule of law. It does so by promoting the revision of existing laws based upon its review of administrative experience. These revisions establish new statutory directives for administrative agencies that may either broaden or narrow their rulemaking authority.

A CLOSER LOOK AT RULES REVIEW AND CORRECTIVE LEGISLATION

The remainder of this chapter presents a case study of the development and use of corrective legislation by JCAR. In particular, the case study focuses on JCAR's efforts to revoke regulations implemented by the Illinois Department of Nuclear Safety entitled "Licensing Persons in the Practice of Medical Radiation Technology." This case study has been selected for several reasons. First, the events leading up to and surrounding the introduction of the revocation legislation into the General Assembly demonstrate the effectiveness of rules review as an information-gathering process and the legislative revision of existing law in light of administrative experience.

Second, this case study shows that the pursuit of corrective legislation is part of the more general rules review process. In particular, corrective legislation is shown to be the logical end product of a rules review process that discovers "abuses" in administrative rulemaking, resulting from initial authority that was either too restrictive, too vague and unclear, or simply violated by a state agency.

In addition, this case study places into a real context many of the observations presented in Chapters 3, 4, and 5. For example, the case study highlights such attributes of rules review as (1) the relationship between a regulation's impact on constituency groups and the relevance of the process to legislators on and off the reviewing committee; (2) its legal and procedural orientation; and (3) the relationship between agency responsiveness and agency costs associated with compliance.

BACKGROUND

In the fall of 1981, WLS-TV, the ABC affiliate in Chicago, aired an investigative report showing that a large number of X-ray machines throughout Illinois had not been inspected in recent years and were miscalibrated. In addition, the news report noted that these machines were frequently operated by persons with little or no training in radiation technology. Individuals requiring X-rays were being exposed to unnecessarily high doses of radiation due to malfunctioning machines and incompetent operators. These high doses of radiation increased the patients' risks of cancer and genetic damage.

In response to the WLS-TV investigative report, the Illinois General Assembly passed and Gov. James Thompson signed into law Public Act 82-901. It amended the Illinois Radiation Protection Act by creating a fee system to cover the cost of inspecting X-ray equipment. The Act also required that all persons administering radiation to human subjects be accredited by the Illinois Department of Nuclear Safety. Finally, the Act created a 12-member Radiologic Technology Accreditation Board that was to advise and consult with the Department on any accreditation plan that was formulated.

To implement the various provisions of PA 82-901, the Illinois Department of Nuclear Safety was authorized to adopt regulations that established a minimum course of education and continuing education for persons employed in the field of radiation technology. These rules were to be consistent with prescribed national health and safety standards necessary for protecting the general public. In addition, the Act directed the Department to grandfather into accreditation all persons who had been employed in the field of radiation technology for not less than 24 of the 48 months immediately preceding January 1, 1984. Those persons were to be grandfathered on the basis of experience and skill. No additional educational requirement was to be imposed upon them. This grandfathering was deemed necessary to prevent practitioners in the rural localities of Illinois from being displaced from their employment by an accreditation program based solely on formal education. These practitioners did not have easy access to radiation technology education programs, and it was feared that requiring training would displace these practitioners, thereby resulting in a lower level of health-care services for rural communities.

Sen. William Marovitz of Chicago introduced the original bill into the Illinois Senate that eventually became PA 82-901. Senate Bill 1492 was extensively debated in both chambers of the General Assembly, and the grandfathering provision of the bill was the focus of most of the discussions. These floor debates reveal a certain amount of confusion over the legislative intent of this provision. In particular, Senator Marovitz and the House sponsor of Senate Bill 1492, Rep. J. Theodore Meyer of Chicago, expressed different opinions as to whether experience and skill were indeed two separate criteria or synonymous. They also disagreed on whether the grandfathering provision was conditional or unconditional.

Senator Marovitz defined experience and skill as one criterion, equivalent to the length of time an individual had been employed in the field of radiation technology prior to January 1, 1984. In response to questions posed by Sen. Roger Sommer of Morton, Senator Marovitz stressed that no additional requirements were to be imposed on those persons then administering radiation to human beings other than their ability to demonstrate to the Department of Nuclear Safety that they had been employed in the field of radiation technology for at least 24 of the previous 48 months. In a follow-up question, Senator Sommer asked Senator Marovitz if his earlier response meant that there would be no change in the status of those persons currently employed in the field of radiation technology. Senator Marovitz responded: "Well, there are people who are not licensed presently to do this and have no training requirements, but . . . if they exhibit to the department that they have been doing this, then they would be allowed to continue to do it without any additional training requirements" (June 28, 1982, 13–14).

Senator Marovitz's intention regarding the grandfathering provision of Senate Bill 1492 was further elaborated in his response to questions pertaining to whether his bill would actually allow incompetent radiation technologists to still administer radiation.

He again stressed that current practitioners would have to verify the length of time they had been employed in the field of radiation technology. In addition, he noted that the persons under whose authority the radiation was being administered would also have to verify that the persons seeking to be grandfathered had indeed been working in radiation technology for the necessary period of time. Though Senator Marovitz believed the supervising authority would have to verify the experience of the practitioners seeking to be grandfathered, Senate Bill 1492 had no such provision in it.

Representative Meyer's understanding of the grandfathering provision was contrary to that held by Senator Marovitz. He stressed both prior experience and skill as necessary conditions for accreditation. He additionally noted that Senate Bill 1492 *did not* provide for the automatic accreditation of those persons then employed in the field of radiation technology. During House debate on the bill, in an exchange that took place between Rep. Judy Koehler and himself, Representative Meyer expressed his understanding of the grandfathering provision: "[T]here will not be automatic grandfathering. . . . The Accreditation Board . . . will determine how much experience and how much skill is necessary for those people to be grandfathered in. . . . You will have to demonstrate to the Board, who will establish the experience and skill criteria" (June 24, 1982, 146–147).

PUBLIC COMMENTS AND REACTIONS

Upon receipt of the legislative mandate in PA 82-901 and the governor's appointment of the Accreditation Board, the Illinois Department of Nuclear Safety began to draft regulations to implement the accreditation provisions of the Act. Working in close conjunction with the Board, the Department filed its first public notice of the proposed rules in the August 5, 1983 issue of the *Illinois Register*. In the proposed radiation technology rules, the Department interpreted the legislative requirement of experience and skill in the grandfathering provision of the Act as separate conditions. This interpretation led the Department of Nuclear Safety to conclude that the General Assembly had not intended an automatic and unconditional grandfathering of those persons then currently employed in the field of radiation technology.

To implement the grandfathering provision of the Act, the Department of Nuclear Safety defined the experience requirement in terms of clinical practice. Clinical practice was defined as the number of months in which the applicant was employed for the express purpose of administering radiation to human beings. The number of months of clinical practice necessary for licensing was the Act's stipulation of not less than 24 of the preceding 48 months. This clinical practice requirement appeared to allow all persons then administering radiation to satisfy the experience requirement. But this section of the proposed rules had a built-in caveat. By counting only months of employment that were for the express purpose of administering radiation, the Department of Nuclear Safety made it more difficult for persons whose work responsibilities only included the occasional administering of radiation to satisfy the clinical practice requirement. This condition potentially impacted upon such persons as industrial nurses who occasionally had to X-ray workers injured in industrial accidents but whose primary responsibilities lay elsewhere.

On advice from the Accreditation Board, the Department operationalized the skill requirement as the license applicant's successful completion of a separate written examination. The examination was to test for the applicant's comprehension of basic skills used in radiation technology. To satisfy the skill requirement, applicants were provided two options: (1) a written examination administered by the Department of Nuclear Safety; or (2) an examination administered by a recognized professional association in the field of radiation technology such as the American Registry of Radiologic Technologists.

To insure that those persons being grandfathered met both the clinical practice and the skill requirements, the Department created a special status of license for them. Grandfathered practitioners who could satisfactorily demonstrate the clinical practice requirement but who could not demonstrate the skill requirement were to be granted a conditional license. Prior to the expiration of the conditional licenses, these grandfathered licensees were still required to pass an examination in order to receive their permanent licenses. Additionally, these conditional licenses were used to insure that no locality in the state was denied adequate health care because of the unavailability of appropriately licensed persons.

As prescribed by the IAPA, the Department of Nuclear Safety provided an opportunity for the affected public to comment on the proposed radiation technology rules. Public comments were solicited through the mail and at one public hearing. In all, the Department received 96 written statements regarding its proposed rules. A Nuclear Safety staff analysis of these comments revealed that 67 percent of the comments were in favor of the proposed regulations. Among those supporting the proposed rules were the two principal state associations in the field of radiation technology: (1) the Illinois Radiological Society; and (2) the Illinois State Society of Radiological Technologists.

The same staff analysis found that only 7 percent of the public comments were opposed to the Department's accreditation scheme. Though direct opposition was low, 27 percent of those who commented on the proposed rules expressed reservations on how Nuclear Safety had interpreted the grandfathering provisions of PA 82-901. Particular concerns were raised over the examination requirement for those persons then currently employed in radiation technology. For example, the Illinois Hospital Association read experience and skill as not requiring additional conditions such as an examination:

> PA 82-901 states that the Department shall provide for accreditation based upon experience and skill. It would appear that the intent of legislation is to provide for a method of grandfathering people who are currently employed in the various specialty areas. The current regulations do not provide for this distinct grandfathering process. A person could be employed by an organization for several years, be competent in the areas, and for a variety of reasons may not be registered. . . . This does not

appear to be totally consistent with the intent of the Act. (Illinois Hospital Association 1983)

Expressing sentiments similar to those of the Hospital Association, one current practitioner, speaking on behalf of 30 of his colleagues, observed: "It was not the intent of the legislators to legislate anyone who had experience and skill out of a job or to put them under hardship. . . . [PA 82-901] does not mean imposing the hardship of a test. . . . [T]he intent of the proposed rules all along has been to put people under a hardship" (Gore 1983).

State legislators whose constituencies were potentially harmed by the proposed regulations also protested the Department's failure to provide unconditional grandfathering. For example, Representative Koehler wrote twice to the Department on behalf of constituents employed in radiation technology. In both communications with the Department, she questioned the proposed rules' implementation of the legislative intent and stressed the presumed hardship that the rules would impose on persons not unconditionally grandfathered. In her September 14, 1983 memo to the Department of Nuclear Safety, Representative Koehler stated: "These requirements seem to violate both the letter and spirit of the law. The education and examination requirement may in fact force many well trained and experienced technicians from the field who are unable to meet the time and expenses required to engage in the courses needed to pass the examination" (Koehler 1983).

Copies of all public comments were provided to the Accreditation Board for its consideration on whether the proposed radiation technology rules should be revised in light of those comments. At its September 1983 meeting, the Accreditation Board rejected the concerns of those who questioned the Department's implementation of the grandfathering provision of PA 82-901. By a unanimous vote, the Board reaffirmed its recommendation to the Department of Nuclear Safety that skill be demonstrated through the successful completion of an examination and that unconditional grandfathering should not be allowed. By disregarding current practitioners' concerns over the grandfathering provision, the Accreditation

Board and the Department, whether knowingly or not, increased the likelihood that JCAR and other legislators would oppose the Radiation Technology rules. By requiring that current practitioners pass an examination, both the Board and the Department were vulnerable to accusations that they ignored the General Assembly's intent in providing a grandfathering provision in PA 82-901 even though this intent was far from being clearly stated by the Assembly.

JCAR'S REVIEW

On November 17, 1983, JCAR's staff formally presented to the Committee the results and recommendations of its review of the Department of Nuclear Safety's proposed Radiation Technology rules. This review consisted of two stages: (1) a preliminary review that was requested by the Department as part of its first notice period of the IAPA; and (2) the standard JCAR review which commenced with the second notice period. In combination, these two reviews resulted in over 200 questions to the Department regarding the radiation technology rules. Thirty-nine percent of all the questions asked concerned issues of regulatory clarity. Policies and procedures questions represented an additional 21 percent of the total, and statutory authority questions contributed another 16 percent of all the questions asked by JCAR's staff.

To resolve the issues raised by these 200 questions, five meetings were necessary between Nuclear Safety and JCAR's staff. Upon completion of the last meeting, the Department's staff was able to report to Nuclear Safety Director Don Etchison that only eight issues remained unresolved. Of these eight issues, JCAR's executive director formally introduced to the Committee six staff recommendations for objections to the Radiation Technology rules. Specifically, JCAR's staff recommended That the Committee object to the Department's proposed rules because Nuclear Safety did not have the statutory authority to (1) require license applicants to take a written examination in order to be accredited; (2) provide for temporary and conditional licenses; (3) exempt students enrolled in radiation technology programs from the accreditation provision of PA 82-901; (4) impose a $25 testing fee in addition to the application fee required by the Act; (5) revoke or suspend licenses once they were issued; and (6) establish a clinical practice requirement as a condition for obtaining a radiation technology license.

These six recommendations for objections represented a basic disagreement between the staffs of the Department of Nuclear Safety and JCAR regarding the scope of authority granted to the Department by PA 82-901. At JCAR's November 1983 monthly meeting, Committee members responded to this disagreement with questions and comments that clearly indicated that they supported their staff's position. Their questions and comments emphasized two areas of concern. First, Rep. Ellis Levin, who had practiced in the areas of administrative and regulatory law, expressed reservations about the overall legal authority of the Radiation Technology rules and their ability to survive court challenges. Though he was critical of the legal authority of the proposed rules, he was in substantive agreement with what Nuclear Safety was trying to accomplish through the regulations:

> My concern is . . . if in fact you do not have the authority, . . . and [you] go ahead with the regs in the form that they're in now, somebody is going to walk into court and they are going to get a TRO [temporary restraining order] not only against part of your proposed regs, which go beyond your authority, but the parts where you clearly have the authority. . . . But, I'd like you to be able to show me that the staff is wrong, and that if in fact you go ahead, you're not going to end up running into a buzz saw in the courts. (November 1983, 23)

The JCAR legislators were also concerned about how the Department of Nuclear Safety was implementing the grandfathering provision of PA 82-901. The Committee members were interested in these provisions of the proposed regulations for several reasons: (1) the committee members believed that the Department may have blatantly disregarded the legislative intent of the grandfathering provision of the Act; (2) the committee members believed that the Department had disregarded negative public comments on how the current practitioners were to be grandfathered; and (3) several of the committee members had received, and were aware that other legislators had received, letters from constituents who would be negatively affected by the proposed grandfathering scheme set forth by the Department of Nuclear Safety. In his statement to the Department's staff, Sen. Arthur Berman expressed these concerns:

> [L]et me strongly suggest one of the things that bothers me . . . when comments from the public were submitted to the Radiologic Technology Accreditation Board, they came down with a unanimous vote that affirmed their position and recommendation [sic] that licensure be by examination and that open grandfathering not be allowed. As I read the debate . . . in the Senate, that is diametrically opposite to how the bill was explained. Now, somewhere, someone either disregarded the debate on the Senate floor, or there was a misunderstanding somewhere, and I'm being gener-ous in that description. (November 1983, 25)

After questioning the Department's staff, the Committee voted to accept all six staff recommendations for objections. The Com-mittee further recommended to the Department of Nuclear Safety that it seek legislation to clarify its statutory authority. On Decem-ber 12, 1983, JCAR received the Department's formal written response to the six committee objections. Nuclear Safety main-tained that it possessed the statutory authority for all provisions of the Radiation Technology rules to which JCAR objected. The Department therefore refused to modify or withdraw any provision of those rules to comply with the Committee's objections. The Department did agree to consider JCAR's recommendation that it seek legislation to more explicitly state its statutory authority.

At its December 1983 meeting, JCAR discussed the alternatives available to it for responding to Nuclear Safety's noncompliance with its six objections. In response to a question by Senator Berman as to what the Committee's options were, Executive Director

Johnson first suggested that if ten members of the Committee were in attendance at the meeting, a Prohibition Against Filing (legislative veto) could be issued against the radiation technology rules. In anticipation of the committee members' interest in this option, the executive director further noted that he had already prepared the paperwork necessary to prohibit the Department of Nuclear Safety from filing those rules with the Secretary of State for their final adoption. If the Department did not file for final adoption prior to JCAR's January 1984 meeting, the prohibition against filing still would remain an option for the committee members to pursue.

Because the Committee did not have three-fifths of its members in attendance, Director Johnson noted that the only option readily available to the Committee was to instruct the staff to draft the corrective legislation necessary to implement the six objections. He added: "To some extent, in order to develop the legislation, we're really talking about implementing legislation to authorize the Department to do what it wants to do" (December 1983, 9). In response to this statement, Representative Flinn, who was then JCAR's chairperson, first suggested the possibility of revocation legislation. Reacting to the executive director's comments, Representative Flinn casually noted: "Or not to do" (December 1983, 9).

The discussion on how JCAR should respond to Nuclear Safety's noncompliance ended with Representative Levin informally requesting that the Committee's staff draft the legislation necessary to implement the six objections "if the Department is not pursuing this" (December 1983, 10). In making this request, his remarks also revealed his hopes that the dispute between JCAR and the Department of Nuclear Safety would not actually have to be fought on the floor of the General Assembly: "I'm sympathetic with an awful lot of what they want to do. Unfortunately, I totally agree that they have no authority to do most of it. And it seems to me to be a tragedy to get involved in this kind of fight when it's going to affect the types [for which] they do have the authority" (December 1983, 10).

Regulating the Regulators

HOUSE BILL 2355

In the latter part of December 1983, the Department of Nuclear Safety filed its notification of final adoption for the Radiation Technology rules with the Illinois Secretary of State. As finally adopted, the regulations contained no modifications responding to JCAR's objections. By filing prior to JCAR's January meeting, the Department preempted the Committee's use of the legislative veto. This action left JCAR only with the option of corrective legislation as a response to Nuclear Safety's noncompliance with its six objections.

At the Committee's January 1984 meeting, Director Johnson presented two recommendations to the committee members for their consideration: (1) that the Committee formally instruct the staff to draft legislation to implement the six objections; and (2) that the Committee request that the director of the Department of Nuclear Safety, Donald Etchison, attend a JCAR meeting in order to more fully explain the Department of Nuclear Safety's position regarding the radiation technology rules. Based upon Representative Levin's informal request at the previous meeting, JCAR's staff had already begun to work with Representative Flinn to draft the now formally requested proposal for corrective legislation. This legislation, which was introduced into the General Assembly as House Bill 2355, sought to revoke the Department's Radiation Technology rules *in toto*—not just the provisions to which JCAR had objected. As one JCAR legislator interviewed for this study observed: "The decision to revoke the entire set of regulations was to attract the attention of the Department and to increase its cost for not complying with the Committee's six objections."

There was no doubt that if House Bill 2355 passed the General Assembly, the Department of Nuclear Safety's ability to implement the accreditation provision of PA 82-901 would be dramatically affected. A fact sheet prepared on April 2, 1984 by the Department's staff determined the immediate impact of House Bill 2355:

The impact of this [House Bill 2355] is to decimate the existing accreditation program by making the Department revoke all 6,000 licenses issued and refund the $160,000 collected. To do this will create considerable confusion in the professional area of medical radiation technology and cost the state the $160,000 collected, plus thousands of dollars in expenses to reverse the present program. (Illinois Department of Nuclear Safety 1984, 3–4)

House Bill 2355 was introduced into the General Assembly to force the Department of Nuclear Safety to comply with JCAR's objections. The bill, however, had just the opposite effect initially. Nuclear Safety hardened its own position and demonstrated its resolve by expediting its clarifying legislation. This legislation sought to grant the Department all the authority it maintained that it already possessed. On April 4, 1984, Rep. Diana Nelson of LaGrange introduced the Department's bill as a floor amendment to House Bill 2355. The Department's substitute bill ultimately failed to be adopted by the Illinois House. But had it been adopted, the amendment would have negated the revocation of the radiation technology rules that JCAR was seeking. In urging her House colleagues to adopt her amendment, Representative Nelson stressed that by granting the Department of Nuclear Safety this additional authorization, JCAR's original request of the Department would be satisfied.

The battle over the radiation technology rules was now being waged on two fronts: in the General Assembly and at JCAR's monthly meetings. At JCAR's April 10, 1984 meeting, Director Etchison testified in order to more fully explain the Department's continued refusal to comply with the Committee's six objections. From the exchanges between the director and the committee members, it was clear that both sides were now entrenched in their positions and that an early compromise was unlikely. The distance between the positions of Nuclear Safety and JCAR was evident in the following exchange between Director Etchison and Representative Flinn:

Director Etchison: At the present time, the law is the law. It took effect January 1, and we have no choice but to implement the law. And the rules are also in effect. Right now we've processed some six to seven thousand applications. . . . We have issued over some five thousand licenses that have been approved. . . . I think the basic question is . . . whether Illinois wants a good program of public health and public safety and to make sure all those people out there administering radiation are qualified. . . . I think we have a realistic program, realistic rules that do that over a phase-in time period.

Representative Flinn: [W]e're arguing about whether the cart comes before the horse or vice versa, and we say to you as an official arm of the legislature . . . that you do not have the authority to promulgate these rules. Go back to the legislature and get that authority lest we strike out all your rules. And that sums up the case, Sir. (April 1984, 4–5)

JCAR and the Department took equally divisive positions on the grandfathering issue, which was clearly the major bone of contention. In stating the Committee's position, Representative Flinn noted:

I think you're going to have a problem when you try to avoid the grandfathering portion of the thing. I'm almost certain that in both houses of the legislature, the hair's going to raise on the back of their necks when they find out you're trying to knock people out of their present positions without grandfathering them in. With the history that we have, you better have a pretty good argument when you get there with that one. (April 1984, 4)

In response to Representative Flinn, Director Etchison noted:

We're trying to protect the public health and safety of the people of this state. Administering radiation to other human beings is a very serious matter. . . . The introduction of the bill to repeal and rescind the rules . . . is like hitting a fly with a sledgehammer. If there is a question about the grandfathering . . . my recommendation is for the legislature to come in with a provision that says "grandfathering." (April 1984, 6)

The battle in which JCAR and the Department of Nuclear Safety were now engaged also included the charade of offering each other "compromises" that neither JCAR nor the Department could accept. For example, at the April 10 meeting, and in a letter to Director Etchison dated the same day, JCAR offered to withdraw House Bill 2355 if Nuclear Safety would repeal the provisions to which the original objections were issued. In a letter to Representative Flinn dated April 24, 1984, Director Etchison rejected this compromise and noted the unrealistic demands that it placed upon the Department:

> For me to comply with that request would essentially nullify all the work that has been done to this point and make the Department licensure program worthless. Indeed, to eliminate the rules would put the Department in violation of the statutory law which mandates that the Department develop rules for the accreditation of all operators of radiation instruments . . . for the purpose of protecting the health of the public. (Etchison 1984)

In responding to JCAR's bad faith compromise, Director Etchison, in his April 24 letter, offered the Committee an equally unacceptable compromise. The director offered to repeal two provisions of the rules that would "not impair our ability to continue the program of regulating radiation technologists." Specifically, Director Etchison offered to repeal those sections of the radiation technology rules that provided for the revocation of licenses and a $25 examination fee. No compromise was offered on the grandfathering issue. To the contrary, his April 24 letter implied that repealing those provisions would impair the Department's ability to protect the public health and safety of the people of Illinois.

With both JCAR and the Department of Nuclear Safety deeply entrenched in their respective positions, Representative Flinn pursued final House action on House Bill 2355. On April 26, just two days after Director Etchison rejected JCAR's compromise, the bill went before the House for its third and final reading. Three JCAR members, Representative Flinn, Olson, and Levin, spoke on behalf of House Bill 2355. In encouraging his colleagues to pass the bill, Representative Flinn stressed the Department's unwillingness to follow the intent of the General Assembly and unconditionally grandfather those persons currently employed in the field of radiation technology:

> They [the Department of Nuclear Safety] ignored the fact that they were not permitting grandfathering in spite of the fact that was one of the main contentions in the original Bill by the House to guarantee that there would be grandfathering of the present people in that business. . . . What it all boils down to [is] that the Department has decided to invoke these rules in spite of the Legislature and in spite of the fact that they don't have the authority. (April 26, 1984, 40)

Representative Olson joined in Representative Flinn's remarks by adding: "What we are facing is an intransigent attitude on the part of the agency in question" (April 26, 1984, 42). In a somewhat more conciliatory tone, Representative Levin again stressed his support for the overall policy the Department was pursuing. Despite his policy congruence with Nuclear Safety, he maintained that House Bill 2355 was necessary to protect the integrity of both JCAR and the General Assembly:

> [T]his is what you might call a "we mean it" bill in terms of protecting the integrity of the General Assembly and of the Joint Committee, that the Department should, in fact, abide by the law. . . . They shouldn't attempt to go beyond it, and we need this legislation passed today to make clear that no agency is above the law. (April 26, 1984, 42)

Only Representative Nelson spoke in opposition to House Bill 2355. Her comments attempted to shift the focus of the debate away from the issue of statutory authority and toward the worthiness of the substantive policy that the Department of Nuclear Safety was pursuing. She asked her colleagues a simple, direct question: "Should we grandfather people who cannot pass [a] test?" (April 26, 1984, 42). She further suggested that revoking the Radiation Technology rules was impractical because of the money that had already been collected and the costs that would be incurred in refunding it and revoking already issued licenses. Representative Nelson's appeal to good public policy and the impracticality of revocation was unpersuasive. House Bill 2355 passed on a vote of 93 "ayes" to 17 "nays."

A LIVABLE COMPROMISE

When House Bill 2355 reached the Illinois Senate, there was little reason to expect that the deadlock between JCAR and the Department of Nuclear Safety could be resolved through further negotiations. But Senator Marovitz, the principal sponsor of PA 82–901, was concerned that if passed in its present form the bill would negatively affect the original intent of the Act. By revoking the radiation technology rules, House Bill 2355 wold not only rescind the accreditation provisions of the rules but also the educational provisions that were clearly intended by PA 82–901. At the request of Senator Marovitz, Senator Bloom, the Senate sponsor, agreed to hold the bill on second reading until an amendment could be negotiated that would not alter the original intent of PA 82–901.

In a process that included both formal meetings between JCAR and Nuclear Safety's staffs and informal bargaining in the halls of the Senate chamber, a compromise amendment was negotiated between Senators Bloom and Marovitz, JCAR, and the Department of Nuclear Safety. Senate Amendment 1 substantially restructured House Bill 2355. No longer did the bill seek to revoke *in toto* the radiation technology rules. Instead Senate Amendment 1 sought to deal specifically with JCAR's six original objections to the rules. The bill now became a clarification of what statutory authority the Department explicitly possessed.

The major compromise worked out in Senate Amendment 1 was the grandfathering issue. Both JCAR's interest in unconditional grandfathering and Nuclear Safety's concern for protecting public health and welfare were represented in the compromise solution. Senate Amendment 1 stipulated that all current practitioners who fulfilled the PA 82–901's experience requirement were to be grandfathered by the Department without taking an examination. On this point grandfathering was unconditional. But there were two caveats attached to this provision of Senate Amendment 1 that satisfied the Department's belief that current practitioners who fulfilled the experience requirement but lacked the necessary skills to safely administer radiation should not be grandfathered. First, before a current practitioner could be grandfathered, the Department of Nuclear Safety had to receive written assurance from the supervising physician or podiatrist that the license applicant had the necessary skills to safety administer radiation to human beings. Second, the licenses of the grandfathered practitioners were required to be specific to the equipment and procedures detailed in the assurance letters.

Senate Amendment 1 was adopted by the Illinois Senate on June 22, 1984, with no serious debate on its merits. Final Senate passage of the restructured House Bill 2355 occurred three days later. Because of Senate Amendment 1, House Bill 2355 was returned to the Illinois House of Representatives for its concurrence in the Senate's changes in the bill. On June 26, Representative Flinn moved for the House concurrence in Senate Amendment 1 and noted: "It very simply settles the argument . . . JCAR had with the Department of Nuclear Safety" (June 26, 1984, 150). The House adopted Representative Flinn's motion and with that concurrence the nearly year-long battle between JCAR and the Department of Nuclear Safety was over. With the passage of House Bill 2355, JCAR's efforts to make the Department of Nuclear Safety accountable were successful. Its interpretation of the legislative intent of the grandfathering provision in PA 82–901 was mostly maintained and substantiated by the General Assembly. As one JCAR legislator observed: "That was all we were really after in the original bill anyway. But the Department was unwilling to compromise so we sought to revoke their rules to get its attention."

7

Summary and Conclusion

INTRODUCTION

In Chapter 1, three basic questions about rules review were put forward for examination: Why is a state legislature likely to adopt a rules review process? What is the substance and the nature of the accountability that a state legislature is likely to seek from state agencies through rules review? What factors are likely to explain agency responsiveness to rules review?

Chapters 3 through 6 have discussed and analyzed these questions within the context of the rules review process in the Illinois General Assembly. From these discussions, a number of analytic generalizations providing an informative introduction to rules review have emerged. These observations also enhance and help shape a broader study of this important and widely used tool of legislative oversight. The purpose of this final chapter is to present a summary of the major analytic generalizations gleaned from earlier discussions and to offer a few concluding thoughts on whether or not rules review is, or can be, an effective means of overseeing and controlling the administrative discretion inherent in redelegated rulemaking authority.

ESTABLISHING RULES REVIEW

Throughout this study, rules review has been presented as a means of overseeing administrative discretion. The Illinois experience with rules review suggests two possible motivations as to why a state legislature is likely to incorporate rules review into its oversight arsenal: (1) to reclaim, and then maintain, lawmaking power lost through redelegation; and (2) to provide relief to affected publics from overburdensome regulations. No assertion is put forth that the two motivations for rules review discussed in Chapter 3 are the only motivations likely to emerge. It is only asserted that reclaiming lost lawmaking power and providing regulatory relief are likely to be among the major considerations that motivate state legislatures to adopt rules review as means of controlling administrative discretion.

The first of these two motivations is most clearly associated with the lawmaking function of a state legislature, and its coordinate concern that majority mandates passed previously by the legislature be faithfully implemented by state administrative agencies sensitive to legislative intent and aware of the boundaries of their statutory authority. In contrast, an interest in rules review for providing regulatory relief is more closely associated with the representative function of a state legislature, and its coordinated concern for articulating the interests of organized groups and the legislators' constituencies. But, as the discussion in Chapter 3 makes clear, these two motivations for establishing rules review are not exclusive of one another. It is highly probable that in advocating the creation of a rules review process, legislators will see the needs for reclaiming lawmaking power and providing regulatory relief as intertwined, and that in preventing major administrative abuses of statutory authority less overburdensome regulations will result.

THE NATURE OF RULES REVIEW

A major purpose of rules review is to hold state agencies accountable for the responsible exercise of their rulemaking authority. But what is the actual substance and nature of rules review? For what and to whom are the agencies held accountable? Any detailed answer to this question will most likely vary from one state legislature to another. But the Illinois experience does suggest an important characteristic that may help to define the nature of rules review in other state legislatures. When pursued by an institutional oversight committee, rules review and the accountability sought through it are likely to appear policy neutral. Policy neutral review does not overtly challenge agencies in regard to the actual substantive content or merit of their proposed regulations. Rather, its focus is more procedural and legal in appearance.

As the comments and actions of the JCAR legislators reported in Chapter 4 suggest, an appearance of policy neutrality will probably develop to reduce opposition from within the legislature toward rules review by creating an impression that the reviewing committee approaches its responsibilities from a narrow and specialized perspective and is sensitive to the will of the whole legislature. But as Chapter 4 also discusses, much of the oversight conducted through rules review will not be neutral. The Illinois experience with rules review suggests three conditions under which presumably neutral review will not actually be neutral: (1) when a proposed regulation becomes salient to a legislator, on or off the reviewing committee, because of the potential impact of the regulation on his or her constituency; (2) when interest groups representing affected publics are allowed to intrude into the rules review process; or (3) when the purpose of rules review is to provide regulatory relief.

The Illinois experience also suggests that the accountability sought through rules review, and the nature of the process itself, are likely to be influenced by a number of informal factors. For example, the accountability sought through rules review is likely to be affected by the manner in which the process is implemented by the legislative agent responsible for overseeing administrative rulemaking. JCAR's review for the statutory authority of proposed regulations illustrates this observation. As the discussion in Chapter 4 points out, JCAR's review for the statutory authority of proposed regulations encompasses a close scrutiny that denies the existence of implicit rulemaking authority. This interpretation leads to a review of proposed rules that looks for all violations of statutory authority, no manner how slight, rather than a review that emphasizes major statutory authority abuses, as was originally intended by the General Assembly.

The relevance that rules review has to other aspects of legislative life for those legislators appointed to the reviewing committee is likely to be the most important informal factor. The Illinois experience suggests that where rules review is conducted by a special institutional oversight committee rather than through preexisting standing committees, the relevance of the process to these legislators is likely to be low. This low level of relevance is also likely to impact upon rules review in several important ways. First, tenure on the reviewing committee will probably be low, thereby decreasing the committee's overall level of expertise and competence. Second, legislators for whom relevance is low will probably participate selectively in the committee's business, withholding their active involvement until such time when rules review becomes infused with their other legislative interests such as constituency service.

Third, the actual legislative responsibilities for rules review will probably become the domain of a small minority of the committee members for whom the process is relevant. Or, finally, the rules review process is likely to become dominated by the committee's staff, with this legislative bureaucracy directly determining the actual substance and nature of the accountability sought from state agencies. In short, the issue of relevance is significant because it is likely to be a major determinant of to whom state agencies are accountable, when they must be accountable, and for what they are accountable.

As just noted, a lack of relevance is likely to lead to a staff-dominated rules review process. Indeed, this is a major conclusion offered in Chapter 4. When rules review is conducted by such a relatively autonomous legislative staff, the manner in which the process is implemented, and therefore also the actual accountability sought from the state agencies, will likely be influenced by other organizational goals of that staff. As Chapter 4 makes clear, much of the rules review undertaken by JCAR's staff appears to be driven by staff management's interest in organizational survival. This goal appears to have produced a sought-after accountability designed to (1) secure JCAR's staff with a clientele other than the General Assembly; (2) neutralize administrative opposition; and (3) promote an impression among the JCAR legislators that state agencies, after more than ten years of legislative scrutiny, still regularly and routinely abuse their rulemaking authority.

AGENCY RESPONSIVENESS

The Illinois experience underscores that the success or failure of an advisory rules review process is likely to depend heavily on the voluntary responsiveness of the state agencies. As illustrated by the low level of responsiveness of Illinois state agencies to statutory authority objections, this responsiveness is also likely to vary across the different types of accountability sought through rules review. The pattern of agency responsiveness to rules review will clearly vary from one process to the next, depending largely upon how the state agencies react to the manner in which rules review is actually implemented. In examining these different patterns of responsiveness, special attention should be given to the level at which state agencies respond positively toward questions regarding the statutory authority of their proposed regulations. If, as in Illinois, a general lack of responsiveness to this component of accountability is routinely discovered, the effectiveness of rules review as a legislative tool for overseeing administrative discretion would clearly be called into doubt.

The Illinois experience further suggests that agency responsiveness to rules review will likely be determined in part by whether or not the state agencies perceive the process to be a credible one. Again, the specific factors contributing to this perception of credibility will likely differ across the various rules review processes. But the Illinois experience with rules review does suggest at least

five factors that may contribute to the credibility of the process:
(1) the level of relevance rules review has for those legislators
serving on the rules review committee; (2) the availability of
sanctions that can be applied, or threatened to be applied, to
unresponsive agencies; (3) the nature of the working relationship
between the reviewing committee and the state agencies; (4) the
reviewing committee's faithfulness to the original intent of the
state legislature when implementing rules review; and (5) agency
costs associated with responsiveness.

The Illinois experience also demonstrates that both a state
legislature and the rules review committee are likely to have some
degree of control over each of these five factors, thereby maximiz-
ing the positive perceptions among state agencies that are necessary for fostering the credibility of the rules review process and
agency responsivenss. For example, to promote a credible process
that fosters agency responsiveness, a state legislature must be
willing to empower the reviewing committee with formal sanctions that can be used against unresponsive agencies. Relatedly,
the legislators on the rules review committee must be willing to
use these sanctions against state agencies. As the impotence of the
legislative veto in Illinois demonstrates, the mere availability of a
sanction is not sufficient. There must also be a genuine threat that
the sanction will be applied before it can promote agency responsiveness. Without the availability of formal sanctions, the rules
review committee must be willing to maximize the coercive powers
of informal sanctions that can be applied elsewhere in the legislative process. Like formal sanctions, the threat or possibility that
informal sanctions will be applied must be genuine in order to
promote agency responsiveness.

A rules review committee can further foster the credibility of
rules review with state agencies through a nonadversarial working
relationship that seeks to minimize agency costs associated with
responsiveness. But perhaps the greatest impact that a state legislature can have on the credibility of a rules review process is by
appointing to the reviewing committee legislators for whom rules
review is likely to be relevant to other aspects of their legislative

life. In particular, state legislative leaders should first select those legislators who are already predisposed toward overseeing administrative behavior and who possess the characteristics attributed to "oversight legislators" (See Chapter 4).

Relatedly, the relevance of rules review, and therefore also its credibility, can be additionally enhanced if the responsibilities assigned to the reviewing committee are oriented toward the two principal legislative functions—lawmaking and representation. Rules review will be relevant to nearly all legislators who serve on the reviewing committee when it focuses upon either major statutory abuses of rulemaking authority, or providing substantive regulatory relief to affected publics. As previously observed, the first corresponds to the lawmaking function while regulatory relief is closely associated with representation.

Major abuses by an agency of its statutory authority should be perceived by many legislators as an affront to the lawmaking power of the state legislature. This will be particularly true for those oversight legislators on the committee. As previously noted, these legislators are already predisposed toward overseeing administrative discretion and protecting the institutional well-being of the legislature. The relevance of rules review should also increase among the non-oversight legislators on the committee. Even these legislators are likely to retain some degree of institutional pride that will be threatened when confronted by major administrative branch abuses of statutory authority. Second, and more important, major abuses of statutory authority are likely to be infused with the opportunity to provide substantive regulatory relief to the affected public. Because regulatory relief approximates the representative function, it will temporarily make rules review relevant to non-oversight legislators. As the case study presented in Chapter 6 clearly documents, providing regulatory relief can allow legislators the opportunity to protect constituency interest, and depending upon the legislators' degree of involvement in correcting the abuse, they may be in the position to claim credit for the resolution of the conflict.

The relevance of rules review to state legislators can be addi
tionally increased if it is undertaken within a structure and in a
manner familiar to the members of a state legislature. In particular,
the relevance of rules review to a state legislator is likely to increase
if it is conducted through existing standing committees rather than
a special joint oversight committee created specifically for that
task. "Standing committee review ... allows the committee which
reported the bill authorizing the promulgation of regulations to
review those regulations" (NCSL 1979, 11). This suggestion is
clearly contrary to current practice. As of 1989, only seven state
legislatures conducted rules review through standing committees.

Advocates of joint committee review argue that the principal
advantages of this structural arrangement are that "the committee's
primary function is regulation review" and a "joint committee may
be more objective in determining legislative intent" than standing
committees would be (NCSL 1979, 12). But a major disadvantage
of the joint committee structure is that the legislators who serve on
it "may have limited knowledge of the substantive areas from
which the regulations are promulgated and they may not be familiar with the development of the language of the enabling law which
determines legislative intent" (NSCL 1979, 12). Without the expertise necessary to review most of the regulations that come
before the joint committee, many legislators who serve on rules
review committees are likely to demonstrate little interest in the
committee's work. Their participation will probably be low, and
they will also likely be heavily dependent upon committee staff
for direction. As Chapter 4 highlights, this is clearly the condition
that prevails within JCAR.

In contrast, standing committee review would expose rules
review to a larger group of state legislators, but would do so within
the context of these legislators' areas of policy expertise. By
definition, standing committee review allows state legislators to
oversee a limited number of regulations, all of which are within
their substantive areas of policy expertise. The very nature of
standing committee review should reinforce the relationship between proposed regulations and their impact upon those areas of

public policy that most interest state legislators. In turn, a clearer understanding of this relationship is likely to increase the relevance that rules review has for these state legislators, as the review of proposed regulations underscores that their responsibilities as legislators do not stop when laws are passed but extend to how those laws are actually implemented by state administrative agencies.

CONCLUSION

In Chapter 2, the dilemma that administrative discretion posed for constitutional government was discussed. The legislative review of administrative rulemaking was also presented as one way in which state legislatures could resolve the dilemma that administrative discretion presents for their constitutional obligation to exercise the lawmaking power of their state governments. It seems only fitting to return briefly to this topic in these concluding remarks.

The basic issue between constitutional government and bureaucracy is not a choice between one or the other, but of blending the two together to provide for a workable system of government. As Maass and Radway (1949, 182) stated: "It is . . . not a question of either democracy or bureaucracy, of either constitutionalism or efficient government [but of] a combination of the two, of a working balance between them, in short, of a responsible bureaucracy." As if to breathe life into these comments, state legislatures have sought to show through the adoption of rules review processes that "[l]awmaking by administrative agencies need not be incompatible with the fundamental principles of . . . [constitutional] government so long as legislatures retain basic control of the process of administrative policy making" (Boyer 1964, 176–177).

Despite the efforts of state legislatures to find a working balance between their constitutional obligations as lawmakers and the necessity for administrative discretion, it remains to be determined if rules review is indeed an effective means of achieving this balance. Most available analyses present a mixed interpretation of its effectiveness. For example, a senior staff associate for the NCSL has concluded:

> "[i]n general ... rules review is an effective means of legislative oversight. Legislators are more aware of the number and substance of regulations being issued by state agencies. ... Gone are the days when agencies could circumvent the legislature with impunity in developing regulations." (Jones 1982, 9)

Among the scant academic assessments, there is a greater degree of pessimism and a more negative evaluation of the capability of rules review to successfully oversee the administrative discretion inherent in rulemaking authority. For example, Ethridge (1985, 156) concluded that, despite political rhetoric to the contrary, "actual experience suggests that the new control mechanisms do not make a legislature capable of bringing large public purposes to bear on implementation questions." To some measure, the analysis presented in this study also addresses the probable ineffectiveness of rules review. For example, the discussion in Chapter 5 on agency responsiveness supports this conclusion.

Whether or not rules review is an effective means of overseeing the administrative discretion inherent in rulemaking largely depends on what the process is expected to accomplish. In turn, any expectations about what constitutes effective rules review must be realistically grounded in the actual powers and authority assigned to it. Since most rules review processes possess only advisory authority, expectations about their effectiveness must reflect this limitation on their power. The case study presented in Chapter 6 suggests that the principal criterion for judging the effectiveness of rules review may be whether or not the process provides a state legislature with the opportunity to retain basic control over the administrative discretion inherent in rulemaking, thereby lessening the dilemma that this discretion poses for constitutional government. The actual opportunities provided through rules review for controlling administrative discretion is likely to depend upon whether the process has advisory or binding authority over proposed regulations.

Because most rules review is advisory, the process itself is unlikely to be suited for serving as the actual legislative agent seeking to secure accountability from state agencies. This is particularly true when the issue involved is correcting an alleged major abuse in an agency's statutory authority or providing substantive regulatory relief. As Chapter 5 makes clear, advisory rules review is not equipped to extract these "pounds of flesh" from state agencies. Rather, as Chapter 6 highlights, advisory rules review provides a state legislature with an opportunity to retain control over administrative discretion by functioning as an information-gathering and reporting process. In this capacity, rules review only identifies and reports to the full legislature areas where agencies have violated their statutory authority, or other areas where rule-making authority may need revising in light of administrative experience.

Through such a narrow role, advisory rules review performs two important functions. First, it clearly provides for some degree of oversight of the administrative discretion inherent in rulemaking. Admittedly, this oversight is far from approximating the actual legislative control of rulemaking authority. Second, by providing information and recommendations to the full legislature, an advisory rules review process can educate state legislators to the importance of revising rulemaking authority in light of administrative experience and making state agencies responsible to the rule of law rather than the vague expectation of informal politics. Once educated, the state legislature as a whole can become the agent through which accountability is actually sought. If advisory rules review is routinely successful at accomplishing these tasks, even in part, it can be judged as an effective weapon in a legislature's oversight arsenal. It will assist a legislature in securing external parity between administrative agencies and itself, thereby lessening the dilemma that administrative discretion poses for constitutional government.

Appendix: Methodological Essay

INTRODUCTION

The research strategy employed throughout this introduction to rules review has been a single-site case study. A respected student of case study methodology recently defined this particular research strategy as a form of inquiry that "investigates a contemporary phenomenon within a real-life context when the boundaries between phenomenon and context are not clearly evident and in which multiple sources of evidence are used" (Yin 1989, 23). Within political science, this case study methodology has a rich and vibrant history. In fact, "the type of study most frequently made in [political science] is the intensive study of individual cases" (Eckstein 1975, 79).

Despite its long tradition within political science, there are many skeptics in the discipline who do not regard the case study methodology (and the field research modes of data collection closely associated with it) as a serious research strategy. It is accused of being something less than scientific, of being a less vigorous form of political science inquiry. This bias appears especially acute among many political scientists who readily embrace every newly available statistical technique.

A common charge made against case study methodology is that it is not possible to generalize from a single case study, or even a multiple case study. As one commentator observed: "The scientific status of the case study is somewhat ambiguous . . . because science is a generalizing activity. A single case can constitute neither the basis of valid generalization nor the ground for disproving an established generalization" (Lijphart 1971, 691).

This criticism is not entirely valid. Scientific generalizations are of two types: from a sample to a population or case studies to a theory. Most critics of the case study methodology recognize only the first kind of generalization. In their shortsightedness, they fail to recognize that a well-constructed case study seeks to generalize to theoretical propositions rather than to a population. "[T]he case study, like the experiment, does not represent a 'sample,' and the investigator's goal is to expand and generalize theories (analytic generalization) and not to enumerate frequencies (statistical generalization)" (Yin 1989, 21). In this regard, one purpose of a case study is to stimulate "the imagination in order to discern important new general problems, identify possible theoretical solutions, and formulate generalizable relations that were not previously apparent" (George 1980, 51).

By stimulating the imagination of the researcher, and hopefully the audience at whom the case study is directed, this methodology makes "an important contribution . . . to theory-building in political science" (Lijphart 1971, 691). In theory building, a case study can best be thought of as a building block on which to construct preliminary theory or a clue as to how a more general model is likely to behave. This is particularly true of a hypothesis-generating case study that seeks to develop analytic generalizations in an area where little or no theory yet exists (Lijphart 1971, 692). Through amendment and refinement, succeeding case studies of other types and varieties improve upon the analytic generalizations set forth in the first. This case-by-case or building-block technique results in a "gradual unfolding" of an increasingly better theoretical understanding of the general phenomenon under study (Eckstein 1975, 104–105).

DATA COLLECTION

Case studies can be built from either quantitative or qualitative data, though the latter appears to be used most frequently in political science. Data for a case study can be collected from at least five sources: interviews, documentation, archival records, observation, and participant observation (Yin 1989, 85). To provide an introduction to rules review, this study has relied principally upon the first two sources of data: interviews and documentation. The following discussion explains how data collected from these two sources were incorporated into the actual study.

Data Collection Through Interviews

Fifty-seven interviews conducted with past and present JCAR legislators, former JCAR staff persons, and representatives from 16 Illinois state executive departments and independent agencies were the first of two principal forms of data used throughout this study. The actual interviewing took place from October 1986 through May 1987, and all persons interviewed were assured anonymity. Most of the interviews were conducted in person, but phone interviews were carried out if the interview subject and I could not arrange an acceptable time or location for an in-person interview.

Fifteen of the 57 interviews were with Illinois state legislators who had served, or were currently serving, on JCAR. These 15 legislators represented 31 percent of all legislators who had served on the Committee as of May 1987. Most of the interviews with the JCAR legislators were carried out in the state capital during the 1986 fall veto session and the 1987 spring session of the Illinois General Assembly. Care was taken to insure that the legislators included in the study represented a cross section of all those who had served on JCAR. For example, among the 15 legislators interviewed were past and present officers of the Committee, committee members with varying tenure, and members who were self-described active and nonactive participants in rules review.

In seeking a cross section of JCAR legislators, both reputation and the availability of the legislators to be interviewed governed much of the sampling. In regard to reputation, it was not uncommon for one JCAR legislator to recommend that I interview another because of that legislator's perceived knowledge or involvement in rules review. When a legislator was recommended frequently, I did try to arrange an interview. In most instances, it was possible to do so.

Availability sampling was necessitated, in part, because the interviews were conducted while the General Assembly was in session. My request for an interview represented just one more intrusion into an already hectic and demanding schedule. Just to complete those interviews with the 15 legislators included in this study took numerous phone calls to their secretaries, countless scheduling and rescheduling of appointments, and a willingness on my part to patiently camp outside their office doors until they had a few minutes to spare for the interview.

Twenty interviews were conducted with former members of JCAR's staff. Locating the whereabouts of former staff presented its own peculiar problems. Because employment at JCAR is perceived by many to be an entry-level position into state government, staff turnover has always been high. At the time this study was undertaken, average staff tenure for rules analysts and staff attorneys was less than two years, and slightly more than 100 persons had gone through JCAR's revolving doors. Because locating the universe of former JCAR staff persons presented an insurmountable task, I decided to interview primarily those former JCAR staff members who were still employed in state government. A list of those persons was drawn from past JCAR payroll records matched against current state payroll records. This list was compiled for me by the Illinois Office of Comptroller.

The 20 former staff persons interviewed represented approximately 21 percent of all persons employed by JCAR from 1978 through October 1986. As with the JCAR legislators, care was taken to insure that those staff persons interviewed also represented a cross section of all persons ever employed by the Committee.

Former staff management, rules analysts, and staff attorneys that made up most of JCAR's 26 person staff were among the 20 former staff persons interviewed. The tenure of those 20 persons ranged from six months to six years, and the time they were employed by JCAR cut widely across the years from 1978 through 1986.

The third group of persons interviewed was 22 representatives from 16 Illinois executive departments and independent agencies. The agency representatives interviewed were responsible for guiding their department or agency's regulations through all or major parts of the rules review process. Specifically, the 16 departments and agencies from which agency representatives were drawn included:

Public Aid	Registration and Education
Commerce and Community Affairs	Nuclear Safety
Children and Family Services	Lottery
Conservation	Transportation
Agriculture	Pollution Control Board
Mines and Minerals	Commerce Commission
Public Health	Health Care Cost Containment Council
Alcohol and Substance Abuse	State Board of Education

These 16 departments and agencies represented a purposive sample. They illustrated all major categories of regulations reviewed by JCAR. In addition, some of the departments, such as the Illinois Department of Public Aid, were included because they were among those departments and agencies that accounted for a major proportion of all rulemaking activity within the Illinois administrative branch of government. For example, the 16 departments and agencies included in the sample accounted for 68 percent of all 1985 rulemaking. These 16 departments and agencies also varied on other important characteristics such as the volume of regulations they issued, whether or not their function was primarily regulatory, and the comprehensiveness of their own internal rulemaking and review processes.

Before leaving this discussion, it is important to note that the quotations attributed throughout the study to the 57 persons interviewed were not verbatim. They were reconstructions from my interview notes. The "quotes" were reconstructed from key terms, phrases, and buzz words used by the subject during the course of the interview. As soon as possible after the interviews were completed, I sat down with these notes and reconstructed the substance of the discussions that I had had with the interview subjects. In reconstructing these discussions, the interviews were written up in chronological order to facilitate my recall so that I could capture the overall tone and emotions of their remarks. Also, when I felt it was necessary, I recontacted interview subjects to insure that I had accurately recorded their comments.

Admittedly, there is a risk of error in the manner in which I reconstructed the interviews. But, in the long run, I believe it was preferable to the alternative of using a tape recorder. First, tape-recorded interviews must still be transcribed, which, in effect, doubles the labor required to collect the data. More important, tape recording interviews has detrimental effects on both the interviewer and the interview subject. In regard to the first, tape-recorded interviews are likely to produce an interviewer who is a lazy listener. In regard to the second, tape-recorded interviews are likely to reduce the candor and spontaneity of the interview subject (Fenno 1978, 279).

Data Collection Through Content Analysis

Content analysis of relevant JCAR and agency documents and publications provided the second major source of data for this study. Content analysis was particularly necessary in building Tables 1, 2, and 4. For example, the question types reported in Table 1 were the result of a content analysis of 1,742 staff questions from 57 rulemakings proposed by the state agencies or reviewed by JCAR in 1985. The year 1985 was chosen because it was the most recent year for which JCAR's review was certain to have been completed and for which the agencies were likely to have the rulemaking files readily available.

The 57 rulemakings were chosen in the following manner. First, only rulemakings from the 16 departments and agencies listed previously were considered for inclusion in the study. Rulemakings from those 16 departments and agencies insured that all types of regulations reviewed by JCAR's staff would be present among the staff questions analyzed. In addition, these 16 insured that those state agencies issuing the major proportion of the 1985 regulations were also included.

Next, a decision was made as to how to select the actual rulemakings on which to conduct the content analysis. This decision was simplified through my interviews with both the agency representatives and former JCAR staff. These interviews all seemed to suggest that there was very little variance in JCAR staff questions across the agencies. These interviews stressed that staff review was very routine and generic. Therefore, in selecting the rulemakings from which JCAR staff questions were to be drawn, the decision was made to focus only on "major" rulemakings— those rulemakings that were likely to have generated staff questions. One indicator of a major rulemaking was whether JCAR issued an objection to it. Twelve of the 16 agencies had objected-to rulemakings. Professional judgment was used to select 26 of these rulemakings.

A second indicator of major rulemaking was nonobjected-to rulemakings that represented new regulations or substantial amendments to existing rules. For a new regulation or proposed amendment to be judged major required that it consist of at least a paragraph of text. Professional judgment was used to select 31 of these rulemakings from the 1985 volume of the *Illinois Register*. The sample of these 57 major rulemakings was distributed across 14 of the 16 agencies.

Once the sample was pulled, I arranged with the various departments and agencies to review the 57 rulemaking files. The documents in these rulemaking files most essential to the content analysis were the General Problems and Questions letters that JCAR sent to the issuing agency after the proposed regulations were initially reviewed by a JCAR staff person. These letters actually listed the questions that JCAR had regarding the newly proposed rules. The questions in these letters were categorized by their substantive content. When questions had multiple parts, each part was treated as an independent question. To promote a greater degree of accuracy, the content analysis on these 57 rulemakings was performed three separate times. The analysis was also guided through discussions with former staff persons who taught me how to read the questions and how to interpret their content to best approximate the meaning that JCAR staff assigned to them when they were originally asked.

Table 2 is also the result of content analysis. The data for Table 2 were obtained from an index of objections maintained by JCAR. Access to this index was obtained through the Illinois Freedom of Information Act. This index listed 29 different types of objections issued by the Committee from 1978 through 1986. Many of these objections had a common denominator and were consolidated into a lesser number of more general types. In Table 2, regulatory clarity was one general type of objection. It included objections that JCAR had indexed as: (1) regulation did not reflect agency policies; (2) agency policies were not in regulation; (3) regulation was not clearly stated; (4) regulation lacked adequate justification; (5) regulation was incomplete; and (6) regulation contained unnecessary language. IAPA general provisions was also a general type. It included objections to regulations that JCAR had indexed as violating provisions of the Illinois Administrative Procedure Act pertaining to general rulemaking, contested case, and incorporation by reference.

Table 4 presents the third major use of content analysis in this study. In it, compliance rates for the combined years of 1978 through 1985 were calculated for 14 of the 16 agencies listed previously. Two of the agencies, the Illinois Department of the Lottery and the Illinois Health Care Cost Containment Council, had not been issued any objections, therefore, compliance rates could not be calculated for them. To obtain the compliance rates for the remaining 14 agencies, all committee objections to their general rulemakings were classified by type and agency response for the years 1978 through 1985. This information was obtained from JCAR's annual reports. Each annual report provided the text of the committee objections and the agencies' responses to them. The actual rates were determined by dividing the combined yearly number of agency modifications and withdrawals by the number of yearly objections to general rulemakings.

Content analysis was also applied to obtain the rates at which the Committee accepted staff recommendations discussed in Chapter 4. These acceptance rates were obtained by analyzing transcripts from 20 JCAR monthly meetings for the years 1984, 1985, and 1986. All staff recommendations to proposed regulations were coded as accepted, rejected, or postponed, depending upon whatever action the Committee took. The transcripts of five monthly meetings were analyzed for each of the years 1984 and 1985. Ten transcripts were analyzed for 1986, which represents the total number of meetings for that year.

THE DYNAMICS OF DATA GATHERING

Anyone who has ever been involved in field research has "war stories" regarding the joy and anguish of data collection. When interviewing is among the principal sources of data, the dynamics of data gathering are likely to center upon access to and rapport with the interview subjects. Access is simply gaining entry into the world of the interview subjects. Rapport is the personal relationship between the interviewer and the interview subjects that encourages the latter to be frank and forthcoming in their remarks. It is essentially the trust displayed by the interview subjects toward the interviewer (Fenno 1978, 263).

The researcher's access to and rapport with the interview subjects are paramount to a successful study. Both are likely to be the result of the researcher's conscious cultivation of the interview subjects, and a large dose of luck. Also, access and rapport are not mutually exclusive. Because researchers are unlikely to be initially known to many of their interview subjects, access obviously precedes rapport. But continued access is likely to depend on building rapport. Access and rapport, or the lack of either, may also impact upon access to other sources of data, such as official documents.

Gaining Access and Building Rapport

In this study, my initial access to and early rapport with the interview subjects appear to have been built on an appreciation for any attention or recognition that this study might bring to rules review, a frustration with the rules review process and a hope that someone would convey this frustration publicly, or empathy with me. The JCAR legislators most frequently displayed the first characteristic. Most seemed to appreciate genuinely that someone was taking an in-depth look at what they believed was an important but not very glamorous aspect of the legislative process in the Illinois General Assembly, a part of the process from which they received little recognition or benefits for their participation.

Access and rapport with agency representatives and former JCAR staff most often appeared based on the second characteristic. Within both groups, there was a high degree of frustration with how rules review was being implemented by JCAR. To relieve this pent-up frustration, most agency representatives and former JCAR staff appeared eager to talk about their experiences with and perceptions of rules review in Illinois.

Frustration and the desire for recognition probably accounted for most of the initial access and early rapport that I had with the interview subjects. For a small minority of these persons, empathy was an additional factor. For example, the research on which this book is based began as my dissertation, a fact that I included in any written correspondence or phone conversation designed to secure access. Several of the interview subjects had advanced degrees in the social sciences, and it is my impression that initial access was granted, in part, because they were familiar with academia. For example, one of the JCAR legislators who was interviewed had a Ph.D. in political science. Similarly, the director of one of the executive departments included in the study also had a Ph.D. In his letter granting me access to his agency, he observed: "As a former Ph.D. candidate myself, I was interested in your letter of January 28. We are glad that you have selected the Illinois Department of _____ for study."

In interviews that typically last only an hour or so, moving quickly beyond initial reasons for access and rapport is essential. Interviewers generally do not have the luxury of building rapport over an extended period of time. Yet they must still behave as if the relationships between the interview subjects and themselves are ongoing. At least in a limited sense they will be, as interviewers find the need to check their interview notes with the interview subjects, arrange follow-up interviews to clarify earlier comments, and insure that the interview subjects are willing to participate in future academic research.

In conducting the interviews for this study, I tried to move beyond the initial access and rapport by allowing the interview subjects the opportunity to talk about themselves, their backgrounds, and how they became involved in rules review. I also assured all interview subjects anonymity. This guarantee was particularly important to the agency representatives who had to maintain a working relationship with JCAR, especially its staff.

Perhaps the most important ingredient in building a lasting rapport with the interview subjects was my effort to convey to them that I was sincerely interested in what they had to say. I tried to underscore that I wanted to learn from them. I stressed that my interest was not in doing a journalistic exposé on JCAR but in using the Illinois experience with rules review to shape ideas as to how a more broad-based understanding of rules review might be achieved. In short, I tried to make myself as nonthreatening as possible.

By taking an "I want to learn from you" approach, I believe that nearly all of the interview subjects were frank and candid in their observations and assessments of rules review and their participation in it. In part because of the rapport that this approach established, several of the interview subjects became "technical advisors" for the research project. This rapport provided me with an important resource upon which to call as I completed the analysis of the data and sought evaluations and criticism of my interpretations.

Access Denied

There are no guarantees that an interviewer will be able to gain access to or build rapport with interview subjects. This "fact of life" became particularly evident to me when I failed to success-fully conclude negotiations with the committee staff management that would have given me access to JCAR's current staff. I attribute this lack of success in gaining access to having been unable to build a rapport with the committee staff management.

I initially requested permission to interview 14 of the 26 staff persons. Committee staff management's initial response was to raise a question regarding the time commitment I was seeking from their staff. Staff management noted that the routine workload of the staff was quite heavy and would not necessarily permit any time to be set aside for interviewing. In an October 1986 meeting, staff management also noted that a large portion of the current staff had been employed with JCAR for a year or less, and they questioned the utility of interviewing these persons. They also raised concerns about the nature of some of my potential interview questions, fearing that published responses could damage the working relationship between the staff and executive departments and the agencies.

In a letter dated October 14, 1986, I formally responded to the staff management's concerns, addressing all points of their reluc-tance to grant me access to staff members. In particular, I offered to interview staff members before the workday started, after work, over lunch, or even over cocktails; reduced the overall number of staff persons I sought to interview from 14 to only those who had been with JCAR for three months or more; and offered to interview staff in pairs or even in threes to further reduce my intrusion into staff's daily routine. In regard to this last concession, I did point out that I thought interviewing staff persons more than one at a time was likely to inhibit their responses and would make my pledge of confidentiality fairly meaningless. A final concession I made to staff management was to offer them the opportunity to review my interview questions in advance and indicate to me any questions that they found particularly disturbing and likely to damage the staff's working relationship with state agencies.

In the last paragraph of the letter, I tried to reassure staff management that my interest in rules review was academic; that I had no interest in doing an exposé on JCAR; and that I represented no threat to either the staff or the Committee. I wrote: "I hope our relationship can be one of cooperation and mutually beneficial. I deeply believe that rules oversight is a topic worth pursuing, but has been sadly overlooked by academics. Your willingness to grant me access to JCAR's staff . . . can help in erasing that neglect."

Eventually, staff management granted me permission to interview seven staff members who voiced an interest in participating in the study. But their names were never supplied to me, nor was I ever able to get staff management to commit to a day and time on which I could conduct the interviews. In our failure to close the negotiations for access, I was left to conclude that staff management was simply reluctant to have either their staff or themselves participate in this study. I attributed this reluctance, in part, to my inability to build a rapport with them.

Impact of Access and Rapport on Other Data Collection

Access to and rapport with the interview subjects can impact on access to other necessary sources of data, such as documents and hearing transcripts, or agency files. For example, my inability to develop rapport with committee staff management greatly inhibited my access to JCAR's files. To gain even limited access to these files, I was eventually forced to invoke the Illinois Freedom of Information Act (FOIA). Relying on the FOIA was something I resisted doing for a long time. Invoking it was an admission that developing a working relationship between staff management and myself would not be possible.

My efforts to gain access to JCAR's files and other relevant documents coincided with those to gain access to current staff members. I was particularly interested in gaining access to JCAR's rulemaking review files to ascertain the nature and substance of rules review. In a December 15, 1986 letter to staff management, I made my original request to review 178 rulemaking files from 13 executive departments and independent agencies. For each department and agency, I specified the exact number of files I wished to review. Only after I sent a follow-up letter one month later did staff management respond to my request. In a letter dated January 23, 1987, committee staff management responded that "it would be impossible to provide the number of files for which you are requesting access due to the staff time necessary to review the content of each prior to providing you with access."

In this letter, staff management offered to consider granting me access to 5 percent of the rulemaking files for 1985, but only after they had "had an opportunity to review [my] revised rulemaking files list." In a letter dated February 11, 1987, I accepted this offer, and I specified the exact rulemakings and their contents that I wished to review. In response to staff management's claim that the files would have to be screened prior to my access to them, I wrote: "Regarding access to these files, I hope we will be able to reach an accord similar to the one I have with the various agencies in my study. Thus far none of the agencies have felt any necessity to screen the files before giving me access to them. . . . [T]he agencies have allowed me total access to their files."

Staff management never responded to my acceptance of their offer. All of the data that described the nature and substance of rulemaking in Illinois was drawn from the rulemaking files of the executive departments and independent agencies included in this study. But there was some information that could only be obtained directly from JCAR. To obtain this information, I made a formal request for access under the Illinois Freedom of Information Act. In a May 15, 1987 letter I wrote:

"Since October 1986, I have corresponded with JCAR's [staff management] on several occasions. Each time I have accommodated [staff management's] request and further narrowed down the information I am seeking to review. My last letter of February 11, 1987 has remained unanswered. Because of this apparent lack of cooperation, I now feel it is necessary to formally invoke the Illinois Freedom of Information Act in order to receive access to the information I need."

There was no longer any reason to believe that a rapport with staff management would ever be developed, and the lack of rapport clearly was a factor in my inability to gain access to other needed sources of data.

In a letter dated May 20, 1987 JCAR's freedom of information officer acknowledged my request and arranged for me to review the files on June 17, 1987. After nearly six months of trying to work with staff management, I was finally gaining some limited access to JCAR's files. In retrospect, I should have filed an FOI request as soon as it became obvious that a rapport with committee staff management would not be forthcoming. But hindsight is, after all, 20/20 vision.

In sharp contrast to the lack of rapport with staff management, my rapport with the agency representatives facilitated access to other data. The agency representatives responded quickly to my requests for access to their rulemaking files. In almost all instances, this access was unrestricted. The only assurance they needed was that any internal memos expressing agency personnel opinions about JCAR would not be directly attributed to the specific individual or to the department or agency from whose file the memo came. In all such matters, they trusted my professionalism.

I can only speculate on the reasons for the vast differences in the access and rapport that I developed with the various groups interviewed for this study and the lack of rapport with committee staff management. Each group was handled in relatively the same manner and, when necessary, I tried to respond to their unique concerns. In the final analysis, access and rapport may be more luck than conscious cultivation. My experiences suggest that an additional factor contributing to gaining access and developing rapport is personality—the personalities of both those persons from whom access and rapport are being sought and the researcher.

EVALUATION OF THE DATA

The broad purpose of this study has been to provide the reader with an introduction to rules review that developed a set of analytic generalizations upon which theory and additional research can be built. An important question worth asking is: Do the data collected for this study allow this goal to be accomplished? I believe that the answer to this question is: Yes, they do. First, the two methods of data gathering routinely complemented and collaborated with one another. For example, in Chapter 4, JCAR legislators spoke openly about how much they depended upon staff for direction. Their rate of accepting staff recommendations for objections, taken from a content analysis of transcripts of the committee's monthly meetings, clearly substantiated this claim and elaborated on it by showing the actual extent to which the committee members are likely to follow staff direction. Similarly, the content analyses of staff questions to the agencies and the index of committee objections substantiated agency representatives and former staff assessments regarding the substance of rules review in Illinois.

Second, interviewing the three sets of principal participants in the Illinois rules review process produced complementing and collaborating data. This was particularly true of the interviews conducted with the former JCAR staff and the agency representatives. On the essentials of rules review in Illinois, their responses and assessments were remarkably similar though admittedly coming from slightly different perspectives. In short, the combination of like interview responses and collaboration across the two methods revealed patterns of regularity that defined rules review in Illinois.

I am convinced that the analysis of the Illinois rules review process is accurate and that the analytic generalizations drawn from it can be part of the foundation on which to build a more general understanding of rules review. But ultimately the judgment is not mine to make. The ultimate judgment rests with those persons who were interviewed and participate daily in rules review and other political scientists who read and react to what I have written here (Fenno 1978, 293).

In regard to the judgment of the participants, I have accomplished my purpose in pursuing this research if I have successfully conveyed their reality of rules review to the reader, if I have revealed how they approach it and think about it. The initial reaction among former JCAR staff and agency representatives who have read all or parts of the manuscript prior to publication and who have called or written to me tell me that I have indeed presented an accurate description of rules review. I do not possess any similar confirmation from the JCAR legislators.

The judgment of other political scientists is the great unknown. How will they judge the data presented within this study and the analytic generalizations drawn from it? Fenno (1978, 294) in the methodological appendix to *Home Style* suggests that to answer my questions, the segment of the political science community to which this study is addressed must answer three questions of their own:

> "Does the description [in the study] ring true ... with whatever experience political scientists have had with people and activities covered in the book?" "Does the study say anything that other political scientists ... might think worth incorporating into their thinking?" "Will political scientists find questions posed [in the study] interesting enough to pick up and pursue?"

I doubt that everyone who reads this book will answer yes to all of these questions. But I hope there are sufficient numbers of political scientists who do answer yes to these questions, thereby demonstrating the contribution this book makes to our understanding of one important aspect of state legislative efforts to oversee administrative discretion. Their affirmative appraisals will also support my belief that, as political scientists, we should seek to record and understand the reality of those persons actually in the game of politics rather than impose our own order on a universe that in actuality may not even be close to being there (Rosenthal 1986, 849).

References

Berger, David G. 1983. Legislative Rules Review in Wisconsin. *State Government* 56 (3): 103–4.

Bloom, Prescott E. 1982. Bureaucratic Overload: Illinois' Legislative Response. In *Legislative Oversight in Illinois*, eds. James Nowland and Anna J. Merritt, 31–35. Zion, IL: Assembly on Legislative Oversight in Illinois.

Bowers, James R. 1988. An Overview of Rules Review in Illinois. *Comparative State Politics Newsletter* 9 (December): 18–26.

Bowsher v. Synar. 1986. 54 USLW 5064.

Boyer, William W. 1964. *Bureaucracy on Trial.* Indianapolis: Bobbs-Merrill.

Bryner, Gary C. 1987. *Bureaucratic Discretion.* New York: Pergamon Press.

Burke, John P. 1986. *Bureaucratic Responsibility.* Baltimore: Johns Hopkins University Press.

Cooper, Joseph. 1985. The Legislative Veto in the 1980s. In *Congress Reconsidered*, eds. Lawrence C. Dodd and Bruce I. Oppenheimer, 364–89. Washington, DC: Congressional Quarterly Press.

———. 1983. Postscript on the Legislative Veto. *Political Science Quarterly* 98 (Fall): 427–29.

Council of State Governments. 1989. *The Book of the States, 1988–1989.* Lexington, KY: Council of State Governments.

———. 1987. *The Book of the States, 1986–1987.* Lexington, KY: Council of State Governments.

De Seife, Rodolphe J. A. 1984. Legislative Delegation of Powers: A Hobson's Choice. *The John Marshall Law Review* 17: 279–307.

Eckstein, Harry. 1975. Case Studies and Theory in Political Science. In *Strategies for Inquiry*, eds. Fred Greenstein and Nelson Polsby, 79–137. Reading, MA: Addison-Wesley.

Elling, Richard C. 1979. The Utility of State Legislative Casework as a Means of Oversight. *Legislative Studies Quarterly* 4 (August): 353–79.

Engles, Michael. 1985. *State and Local Politics: Fundamentals and Perspectives*. New York: St. Martin's Press.

Etchinson, Donald. 1984. Letter to Rep. Monroe Flinn, 24 April. Copy on file with the Illinois Department of Nuclear Safety, Springfield. Licensing of persons in the practice of medical radiation technology, 32 Ill. Admin. C., sec. 401.

Ethridge, Marcus E. 1985. *Legislative Participation in Implementation*. New York: Praeger.

———. 1984a. Consequences of Legislative Review of Agency Regulations in Three States. *Legislative Studies Quarterly* 9 (February): 161–78.

———. 1984b. A Political-Institutional Interpretation of Legislative Oversight Mechanisms and Behavior. *Polity* 17 (Winter): 340–59.

Fenno, Richard F., Jr. 1978. *Home Style*. Boston: Little, Brown.

———. 1973. *Congressmen in Committee*. Boston: Little Brown.

Finer, Herman. 1941. Administrative Responsibility in Democratic Government. *Public Administration Review* 1 (Summer): 335–50.

Fisher, Louis. 1986. The Administrative State: What's Next after Chadha and Bowsher? Paper presented at the 1986 American Political Science Association Meeting, Washington, DC.

———. 1985. *Constitutional Conflicts Between Congress and the President*. Princeton, NJ: Princeton University Press.

Franklin, Daniel Paul. 1986. Why the Legislative Veto Isn't Dead. *Presidential Studies Quarterly* 16 (Summer): 491–502.

Freedman, James O. 1978. *Crisis and Legitimacy*. Cambridge: Cambridge University Press.

Friedrich, Carl J. 1968. *Constitutional Government and Democracy*. Waltham, MA: Blaisdell Publishing.

George, Alexander L. 1980. Case Studies and Theory Development. In *Diplomacy: New Approaches in History, Theory, and Policy*, ed. Paul G. Lauren, 43–68. New York: Free Press.

Gilmour, Robert S. 1982. The Congressional Veto: Shifting the Balance of Administrative Control. *Journal of Policy Analysis and Management* 2: 13–25.

Gore, Delbert. 1983. Written testimony provided to the Illinois Department of Nuclear Safety at 14 June public hearing in Springfield. Copy on file with the Illinois Department of Nuclear Safety, Springfield. Licensing of persons in the practice of medical radiation technology, 32 Ill. Admin. C., sec. 401.

Gruber, Judith E. 1987. *Controlling Bureaucracies.* Berkeley: University of California Press.

Haltom, William. 1989. Separating Powers: Dialectical Sense and Positive Nonsense. In *Judging the Constitution*, eds. Michael W. McCann and Gerald L. Houseman, 127–53. Glenview, IL: Scott, Foresman.

Hamm, Keith E. and Roby D. Robertson. 1981. Factors Influencing the Adoption of Legislative Oversight in the United States. *Legislative Studies Quarterly* 6 (February): 133–50.

Harris, Joseph P. 1964. *Congressional Control of Administration.* Washington, DC: Brookings Institution.

House Democratic Staff, Illinois General Assembly. 1976. *Administrative Rules and Regulations.* Nonpublished internal legislative study located in the private files of Ken Mitchell, former JCAR assistant director, Springfield.

Illinois Administrative Procedure Act. 1986. *Illinois Revised Statutes.* Chap. 127, par. 1001–21.

Illinois Department of Nuclear Safety. 1984. *Fact Sheet on House Bill 2355.* Copy on file with the Illinois Department of Nuclear Safety, Springfield. Licensing of persons in the practice of medical radiation technology, 32 Ill. Admin. C., sec. 401.

Illinois General Assembly. 1984. House and Senate legislative debate on House Bill 2355. 84th General Assembly, 1984 session. Copy on file with the Illinois Secretary of State, Index Division, Springfield.

———. 1982a. House and Senate legislative debate on Senate Bill 1492. 82nd General Assembly, 1982 session. Copy on file with the Illinois Secretary of State, Index Division, Springfield.

———. 1982b. House and Senate legislative debate on House Bill 834. 82nd General Assembly, 1982 session. Copy on file with the Illinois Secretary of State, Index Division, Springfield.

———. 1980a. House and Senate legislative debate on Senate Bill 1822. 81st General Assembly, 1980 session. Copy on file with the Illinois Secretary of State, Index Division, Springfield.

———. 1980b. House and Senate legislative debate on House Bill 1503. 81st General Assembly, 1980 session. Copy on file with the Illinois Secretary of State, Index Division, Springfield.

———. 1980c. House and Senate legislative debate on House Bill 2351. 81st General Assembly, 1980 session. Copy on file with the Illinois Secretary of State, Index Division, Springfield.

———. 1979. House and Senate legislative debate on Senate Bill 307. 81st General Assembly, 1979 session. Copy on file with the Illinois Secretary of State, Index Division, Springfield.

———. 1977. House and Senate legislative debate on House Bill 14. 80th General Assembly, 1977 session. Copy on file with the Illinois Secretary of State, Index Division, Springfield.

Illinois Hospital Association. 1983. Written testimony provided to the Illinois Department of Nuclear Safety at 14 June public hearing in Springfield. Copy on file with the Illinois Department of Nuclear Safety, Springfield. Licensing of persons in the practice of medical radiation technology, 32 Ill. Admin. C., sec. 401.

Immigration and Naturalization Service v. Chadha. 1983. 462 U.S. 919.

Jewell, Malcolm E. and Samuel C. Patterson. 1977. *The Legislative Process in the United States.* New York: Random House.

Johnson, Bruce. 1985. General Problem and Question letter to Kathy Campbell Lynch, 19 June. Copy on file with the Illinois Department of Registration and Education, Springfield. Public Accounting Act, 68 Ill. Admin. C., sec. 402.56, 420.65.

Johnson, Steve F. 1983. The Legislative Veto in the States. *State Government* 56 (3): 99–102.

Joint Committee on Administrative Rules, Illinois General Assembly. 1987. *1986 Annual Report to the Illinois General Assembly.* Springfield, IL: Joint Committee on Administrative Rules.

———. 1986a. *1985 Annual Report to the Illinois General Assembly.* Springfield, IL: Joint Committee on Administrative Rules.

———. 1986b. Transcripts of JCAR monthly meetings (August and December). Copy on file with the Joint Committee on Administrative Rules, Springfield.

———. 1984a. *1983 Annual Report to the Illinois General Assembly.* Springfield, IL: Joint Committee on Administrative Rules.

———. 1984b. Transcripts of JCAR monthly meetings (April). Copy on file with the Joint Committee on Administrative Rules, Springfield.

———. 1983a. Transcripts of JCAR monthly meetings (November and December). Copy on file with the Joint Committee on Administrative Rules, Springfield.

———. 1983b. Untitled internal staff task force report. Copy obtained from the private files of a former JCAR staff member who wished to remain anonymous.

———. 1982. *1981 Annual Report to the Illinois General Assembly.* Springfield, IL: Joint Committee on Administrative Rules.

———. 1981. *1980 Annual Report to the Illinois General Assembly.* Springfield, IL: Joint Committee on Administrative Rules.

———. 1980. *1979 Annual Report to the Illinois General Assembly*. Springfield, IL: Joint Committee on Administrative Rules.

———. 1979. *1978 Annual Report to the Illinois General Assembly*. Springfield, IL: Joint Committee on Administrative Rules.

Jones, Rich. 1982. Legislative Review of Regulations: How Well Is It Working? *State Legislatures* 8 (September): 7–9.

Keefe, William and Morris Ogul. 1981. *The American Legislative Process*. Englewood Cliffs, NJ: Prentice-Hall.

Koehler, Judy. 1983. Memo to the Illinois Department of Nuclear Safety, 12 September. Copy on file with the Illinois Department of Nuclear Safety, Springfield. Licensing of persons in the practice of medical radiation technology, 32 Ill. Admin. C., sec. 401.

Krislov, Samuel and David H. Rosenbloom. 1981. *Representative Bureaucracy and the American Political System*. New York: Praeger.

Landis, James M. 1938. *The Administrative Process*. New Haven, CT: Yale University Press.

Legislative Council, Illinois General Assembly. 1976. *Legislative Delegation of Rulemaking Authority in Illinois Statutes*. File 8–680.

Legislative Research Unit, Illinois General Assembly. 1984. *Preface to Lawmaking*. Springfield, IL: Legislative Research Unit.

Legislative Study Group, Maryland General Assembly. 1977. *The Joint Legislative Committee on Administrative and Legislative Review: Its Past Procedures and Proposals for Change*. Annapolis, MD: Legislative Study Group.

Lijphart, Arend. 1971. Comparative Politics and the Comparative Method. *American Political Science Review* 65: 682–93.

Lowi, Theodore J. 1979. *The End of Liberalism*. New York: Norton.

Lyons, William and Larry W. Thomas. 1978. *Oversight in State Legislatures*. Knoxville: Bureau of Public Administration, University of Tennessee.

Maass, Arthur. 1983. *Congress and the Common Good*. New York: Basic Books.

Maass, Arthur and Laurence I. Radway. 1949. Gauging Administrative Responsibility. *Public Administration Review* 9 (Summer): 182–93.

MacIntyre, Angus A. 1986. The Multiple Sources of Statutory Ambiguity: Tracing the Legislative Origins to Administrative Discretion. In *Administrative Discretion and Public Policy Implementation*, eds. Douglas H. Shumavon and H. Kenneth Hibbeln, 67–88. New York: Praeger.

Mahoney, Mitzi. 1985. Legislative Oversight of Administrative Policy Making. Paper presented at the 1985 American Political Science Association Meeting, New Orleans, Louisiana.

Malbin, Michael. 1980. *Unelected Representatives*. New York: Basic Books.

McCubbins, Matthew P. and Thomas Schwartz. 1984. Congressional Oversight Overlooked. *American Journal of Political Science* 28 (February): 167–79.

Miller, Cheryl M. 1987. The Politics of Legislative Curtailment of Administrative Rulemaking. *Policy Studies Review* 6 (May): 631–43.

Mosher, Frederick E. 1982. *Democracy and the Public Service.* 2nd ed. New York: Oxford University Press.

Nachmias, David and David H. Rosenbloom. 1980. *Bureaucratic Government USA.* New York: St. Martin's Press.

National Conference of State Legislatures. 1980. Legislative Veto. *State Legislative Report* 5 (October): 1–5.

———. 1979. *Restoring the Balance in the Legislative Review of Administrative Regulations.* Denver: National Conference of State Legislatures.

Ogul, Morris J. 1976. *Congress Oversees the Bureaucracy.* Pittsburgh: University of Pittsburgh Press.

Powell, Norman John. 1967. *Responsible Bureaucracy in the United States.* Boston: Allyn and Bacon.

Pritchett, C. Herman. 1984. *Constitutional Law of the Federal System.* Englewood Cliffs, NJ: Prentice-Hall.

———. 1968. *The American Constitution.* New York: McGraw-Hill.

Proffer, Lanny. 1984. Legislative Veto Alternatives. *State Legislatures* 10 (January): 23–25.

Riley, Dennis R. 1987. *Controlling the Federal Bureaucracy.* Philadelphia: Temple University Press.

Ripley, Randall B. 1983. *Congress: Process and Policy.* 3rd ed. New York: Norton.

Rohr, John A. 1986. *To Run a Constitution.* Lawrence: University of Kansas Press.

Rosen, Bernard. 1982. *Holding Government Bureaucrats Accountable.* New York: Praeger.

Rosenbloom, David H. 1989. *Public Administration: Understanding Management, Politics, and Law in the Public Sector.* New York: Random House.

———. 1983. *Public Administration and Law.* New York: Marcel Dekker.

Rosenthal, Alan. 1986. Soaking, Poking, and Wallowing in It. *PS* 19 (Fall): 845–50.

———. 1981a. Legislative Behavior and Legislative Oversight. *Legislative Studies Quarterly* 7 (February): 115–31.

———. 1981b. *Legislative Life.* New York: Harper and Row.

Rossiter, Clinton, ed. 1961. *The Federalist Papers.* New York: Mentor Books.

Schechter Poultry Corp. v. United States. 1935. 295 U.S. 495.

Schubert, Glendon A. 1958. Legislative Adjudication of Administrative Legislation. *Journal of Public Law* 7 (Spring): 135–61.

Shumavon, Douglas H. and H. Kenneth Hibbeln. 1986. *Administrative Discretion and Public Policy Implementation.* New York: Praeger.

Smith, Steven S. and Christopher J. Deering. 1984. *Committees in Congress.* Washington, DC: Congressional Quarterly Press.

Spiro, Herbert J. 1969. *Responsibility in Government.* New York: Van Nostrand Reinhold.

Starr, C. M. III. 1980. California's New Office of Administrative Law and Other Amendments to the California APA. *Administrative Law Review* 32 (Fall): 713–32.

State Government Committee, Pennsylvania General Assembly, Senate. 1986. *The Chairman's Report on Regulatory Review.* Harrisburg, PA: State Government Committee.

Sundquist, James. 1981. *The Decline and Resurgence of Congress.* Washington, DC: Brookings Institution.

Van Der Slik, Jack R. and Kent D. Redfield. 1986. *Lawmaking in Illinois.* Springfield, IL: Office of Public Affairs Communication, Sangamon State University.

Webb, Ernest. 1986. Letter to Bruce Johnson, 6 August. Copy on file with the Illinois Department of Children and Family Services, Springfield. Transracial Adoptions, 89 Ill. Admin. C., sec. 302.20, 302.300, 302.390.

West, William F. 1985. *Administrative Rulemaking.* Westport, CN: Greenwood Press.

———. 1984. Structuring Administrative Discretion: The Pursuit of Rationality and Responsiveness. *American Journal of Political Science* 28 (May): 340–60.

West, William F. and Joseph Cooper. 1989. The Context of Administration and the Control of Bureaucratic Discretion. Paper presented at the 1989 Midwest Political Science Association Meeting, Chicago, Illinois.

Yin, Robert K. 1989. *Case Study Research*, 2nd ed. Newbury Park, CA: Sage Publications.

Youngstown Steel Co. v. Sawyer. 1952. 343 U.S. 579.

Yourell, Harry. 1976. Statement to the House Executive Committee. In *Administrative Rules and Regulations*, House Democratic Staff, Illinois General Assembly.

Index

About the Author

JAMES R. BOWERS is an assistant professor of political science at St. John Fisher College, Rochester, New York. His publications include "Agency Responsiveness to the Legislative Oversight of Administrative Rulemaking" and "An Overview of Rules Review in Illinois."